waiting on
GOD

Andrew Murray

Whitaker House

WAITING ON GOD

ISBN: 0-88368-101-3
Printed in the United States of America
© 1981, 1983 by Whitaker House

Whitaker House
30 Hunt Valley Circle
New Kensington, PA 15068
web site: www.whitakerhouse.com

15 16 17 18 19 20 21 22 / 09 08 07 06 05 04 03 02

CONTENTS

FOREWORD

Before my trip to England, I had been very impressed by the thought of how, in all our Christianity, personal and public, we need more of God. I felt that we needed to train our people to wait on God more, to cultivate a deeper sense of His presence, to seek more direct contact with Him, and to rest in entire dependence on Him. These must be the definite aims of our ministry. At a "welcome" breakfast in Exeter Hall, I expressed this thought very simply in connection with all our spiritual work. I have already said elsewhere that I was surprised at the response the sentiment met with. I saw that God's Spirit had been working the same desire in many hearts.

The experiences of the past year, both personal and public, have greatly deepened the conviction. It is as if I myself am only beginning to see the deepest truth concerning God and our relationship to Him. It must be centered in this waiting on God, and how very little, in our life and work, we have been surrounded by its spirit. The following pages are the outcome of my conviction and of desire to direct the attention of all God's people to the one great remedy for all our needs. More than half the pieces were written on board ship. I fear they bear the marks of being somewhat crude and hasty. I have felt that I should write them over again. But, this I cannot do now. And so, I send them out with the prayer that He who loves to use the feeble may give His blessing with them.

I do not know if it will be possible for me to put into a few words the chief things we need to learn. But, what I want to say here is this: The great lack of our faith is that *we do not know God*. The answer to every complaint of feebleness and failure, the message to every congregation or convention seeking instruction on holiness, ought to simply be, What is the matter: *Have you not God?* If you really believe in God, He will make everything all right. God is willing and able by His Holy Spirit. Cease from expecting the least good from yourself, or the least help from anything there is in man. Just yield yourself unreservedly to God to work in you. He will do all for you.

How simple this looks! And yet, this is the gospel we so little know. I feel ashamed as I send forth these very defective teachings; I can only cast them on the love of my brethren, and of our God. May He use them to draw us all to Himself, to learn in practice and experience the blessed art of *waiting only upon God*. If only God would show us the right conception of what the influence would be on a life spent, not in thought or imagination or effort, but in the power of the Holy Spirit, wholly waiting upon God.

With my greeting in Christ to all God's saints it has been my privilege to meet, and no less to those I have not met, I subscribe myself, your brother and servant,

Andrew Murray

waiting on GOD

Chapter 1

THE GOD OF OUR SALVATION

"My soul waiteth only upon God; from him cometh my salvation"—Psalm 62:1 (A.S.V.).

If salvation truly comes from God and is entirely His work, just as our creation was, it follows that our first and highest duty is to wait on Him and to do that work which pleases Him. Waiting then becomes the only way to the experience of a full salvation— the only way to truly know God as the God of our salvation. All the difficulties which are brought forward, as keeping us back from full salvation, have their cause in this one thing: the defective knowledge and practice of waiting upon God. All that the Church and its members need for the manifestation of the mighty power of God in the world is the return to our true place, the place that belongs to us, both in creation and redemption, the place of absolute and unceasing dependence upon God. Let us strive to see what elements make up this most blessed and necessary waiting upon God. It may help us if we discover the reasons why this grace is so little cultivated. We must feel how infinitely desirable it is that the Church, that we ourselves, should learn its blessed secret at any price.

The deep need for this waiting on God lies equally in the nature of man and the nature of God. God, as Creator, formed man to be a vessel in which He could show forth His power and goodness. Man was not to have, in himself, a fountain of life or strength or happiness. The ever-living and only living One was to each moment communicate to man all that he needed. Man's glory and blessedness was not to be independent, or dependent upon himself, but dependent on a God of such infinite riches and love. Man was to have the joy of constantly receiving from the fullness of God. This was his blessedness as an unfallen creature.

When he fell from God, he was still more absolutely dependent on Him. There was not the slightest hope of his recovery out of his state of death, but in God, His power and mercy. It is God alone who began the work of redemption. It is God alone who continues and carries it on each moment in each individual believer. Even in the regenerate man, there is no power of goodness in himself. He has and can have nothing that he does not each moment receive. Waiting on God is just as indispensable, and must be just as continuous and unbroken, as the breathing which maintains his natural life.

It is then because Christians do not know their relationship to God as absolute poverty and helplessness, that they have no sense of the need of absolute and unceasing dependence, or of the unspeakable blessedness of continually waiting on God. But, once a believer begins to see it and consent to it—that he must, by the Holy Spirit, each moment receive what God each moment works—waiting on God becomes his brightest hope and joy. As he begins to understand how God, as God, as infinite Love, delights to impart His own nature to His child as fully as He can—how God is not weary of keeping charge of his life and strength—he wonders why he ever thought that God could not be waited on all day. God unceasingly giving and working and His child unceasingly waiting and receiving; this is the blessed life.

"Truly my soul waiteth upon God; from Him cometh my salvation." First, we wait on God for salvation. Then, we learn that salvation is only to bring us to God and teach us to wait on Him. Then, we find what is better still, that waiting on God is itself the highest salvation. It is ascribing to Him the glory of being All; it is experiencing that He is All to us. May God teach us the blessedness of waiting on Him!

My soul, wait thou only upon God!

16/5

15/6

Chapter 2

THE KEYNOTE OF LIFE

"I have waited for thy salvation, O Lord"—
Genesis 49:18.

It is not easy to say in what exact sense Jacob used these words in the midst of his prophecies in regard to the future of his sons. But, they certainly do indicate that, both for himself and for them, his expectation was from God alone. It was God's salvation he waited for; a salvation which God had promised and which God Himself alone could work out. He knew himself and His sons to be under God's charge. Jehovah the everlasting God would show them what His saving power is and does. The words point forward to that wonderful history of redemption which is not yet finished, and to the glorious future in eternity to which it is leading. They suggest to us how there is no salvation but God's salvation, and how waiting on God for that, whether for our personal experience or in wider circles, is our first duty, our true blessedness.

Let us think of ourselves and the inconceivably glorious salvation God has worked out for us in Christ and is now going to perfect in us by His Spirit. Let us meditate until we realize that every participation of this great salvation, from moment to moment, must be the work of God Himself. God cannot part with His grace or goodness or strength as an external thing that He gives us, as He gives the raindrops from heaven. No, He can only give it, and we can only enjoy it, as He works it Himself directly and unceasingly. And, the only reason that He does not work it more effectually and continuously is that we do not let Him. We hinder Him either by our indifference or by our self-effort, so that He cannot do what He wants to do.

What He asks of us, in the way of surrender, obedience, desire, and trust, is all comprised in this one word: waiting on Him, waiting for His salvation. It combines the deep sense of our entire helplessness and our perfect confidence that our God will work all in His divine power.

Again, I say, let us meditate on the divine glory of the salvation God purposes to work out in us, until we know the truths it implies. Our heart is the scene of a divine operation more wonderful than Creation. We can do as little toward the work as toward creating the world, except as God works in us to will and to do. God only asks us to yield, to consent, to wait upon Him, and He will do it all. Let us meditate and be still, until we see how right and blessed it is that God alone do all. Our soul will, of itself, sink down in deep humility to say: "I have waited for Thy salvation, O Lord." And the deep blessed background of all our praying and working will be: "Truly my soul waiteth upon God."

The application of the truth to wider circles, to those we labor among or intercede for, to the Church of Christ around us, or throughout the world, is not difficult. There can be no good but what God works. To wait upon God, and have the heart filled with faith in His working, and in that faith to pray for His mighty power to come down, is our only wisdom. Oh, for the eyes of our heart to be opened to see God working in ourselves and in others. If only we could see how blessed it is to worship and to wait for His salvation!

Our private and public prayers are our chief expressions of our relationship to God. It is in them chiefly that our waiting upon God must be exercised. If our waiting begins by quieting the activities of nature, and being still before God; if it bows and seeks to see God in His universal and almighty operation, alone able and always ready to work all good, then it will be the strength of the soul. If it yields itself to Him in the assurance that He is working and will work in us; if it maintains the place of humility and stillness, and surrenders until God's Spirit has quickened the faith that He will perfect His work, it will indeed become the joy of the soul. Life will become one deep, blessed cry: "I have waited for Thy salvation, O Lord."

My soul, wait thou only upon God!

Chapter 3

THE TRUE PLACE OF MAN

"These wait all upon thee, That thou mayest give them their meat in due season. That thou givest unto them, they gather; Thou openest thine hand, they are satisfied with good"—Psalm 104:27,28 (A.S.V.).

This psalm, in praise of the Creator of the birds and the beasts of the forest, of the young lions, and man going forth to his work, of the great sea, where things exist, both small and great beasts. And, it sums up the whole relationship of all creation to its Creator, and its continuous and universal dependence upon Him in the one word: "These all wait upon Thee!" Just as much as it was God's work to create, it is His work to maintain. As little as man could create himself, is he left to provide for himself. The whole creation is ruled by the one unalterable law of *waiting upon God!*

The word is the simple expression of that for the sake of which alone man was brought into existence, the very groundwork of his constitution. The one

19

object for which God gave life to mankind was that in them He might prove and show forth His wisdom, power, and goodness. He would be, each moment, their life and happiness, and pour forth unto them the riches of His goodness and power. And just as this is the very place and nature of God, to be unceasingly the supplier of every want, so the very place and nature of man is nothing but this—to wait upon God and receive from Him what He alone can give, what He delights to give.

If we are at all to understand what *waiting on God* is to be to the believer, to practice it and to experience its blessedness, it is of great importance that we begin at the very beginning and see the deep reasonableness of the call that comes to us. We will then understand how the duty is no arbitrary command. We will see how it is not only rendered necessary by our sin and helplessness. It is simply and truly our restoration to our original destiny and our highest nobility, to our true place and glory as people blessedly dependent on the All-glorious God.

Once our eyes are opened to this precious truth, all nature will become a preacher, reminding us of the relationship which, founded in creation, is now taken up in grace. As we read this psalm, and learn to look upon all life in nature as continually maintained by God Himself, waiting on God will be seen to be the very necessity of our being. As we think of the young lions and the ravens crying to Him, of the birds and the fishes and every insect waiting on Him, until He gives them their meat in due season, we will see that it is the very nature and glory of God that He is a God who is to be waited on. Every thought of what nature is, and of what God is, will give new force to the call: "Wait thou only upon God."

"These all wait upon Thee, that Thou mayest *give.*" It is God who gives all: let this faith enter deeply into our hearts. Before we fully understand all that is implied in our waiting upon God, and before we have even been able to cultivate the habit, let the truth enter our souls. Waiting on God, unceasing and entire dependence upon Him, is, in heaven and earth, the only true faith, the one unalterable and all-comprehensive expression for the true relationship to the ever-blessed One in whom we live.

Let us resolve at once that it will be the one characteristic of our life and worship, a continual, humble, truthful waiting upon God. We may rest assured that He who made us for Himself, that He might give Himself to us and in us, that *He* will never disappoint us. In waiting on Him, we will find rest and joy and strength, and the supply of every need.

My soul, wait thou only upon God!

Chapter 4

FOR SUPPLIES

"The Lord upholdeth all that fall, And raiseth up all those that be bowed down. The eyes of all wait upon thee; And thou givest them their meat in due season"—Psalm 145:14,15.

Psalm 104 is a psalm of Creation, and the words, "These all wait upon Thee," were used with reference to the animal creation. Here, we have a psalm of the Kingdom, and "the eyes of all wait upon Thee" appears specially to point to the needs of God's saints, of all who fall and are heavy laden. What the universe and the animal creation does unconsciously, God's people are to do intelligently and voluntarily. Man is to be the interpreter of nature. He is to prove that there is nothing nobler or more blessed in the exercise of our free will than to use it in waiting upon God.

If any army has been sent out to march into an enemy's country, and news is received that it is not advancing, the question is at once asked, what is the cause of the delay. The answer will very often be:

"Waiting for supplies." All the stores of provisions or clothing or ammunition have not arrived. Without these, it dare not proceed. It is likewise in the Christian life: day by day, at every step, we need our supplies from above. And, there is nothing so necessary as to cultivate that spirit of dependence on God and of confidence in Him, which refuses to go on without the needed supply of grace and strength.

If the question is asked, whether this is anything different from what we do when we pray, the answer is that there may be much praying with very little waiting on God. In praying, we are often occupied with ourselves, with our own needs, and our own efforts in the presentation of them. In waiting upon God, the first thought is of *the God upon whom we wait*. We enter His presence, and feel we need just to be quiet, so that He, as God, can overshadow us with Himself. God longs to reveal Himself, to fill us with Himself. Waiting on God gives Him time in His own way and divine power to come to us.

It is especially at the time of prayer that we ought to set ourselves to cultivate this spirit.

Before you pray, bow quietly before God, just to remember and realize who He is, how near He is, how certainly He can and will help. Just be still before Him, and allow His Holy Spirit to waken and stir in your soul the childlike disposition of absolute dependence and confident expectation. Wait upon God as a living Being, as the living God, who notices you. He is just longing to fill you with His salvation. Wait on God until you know you have met Him;

prayer will then become so different.

And when you are praying, let there be intervals of silence, reverent stillness of soul, in which you yield yourself to God, in case He may have other things He wishes to teach you or to work in you. Waiting on Him will become the most blessed part of prayer, and the blessing thus obtained will be doubly precious as the fruit of such fellowship with the Holy One. God has so ordained it, in harmony with His holy nature, and with ours, that waiting on Him should be the honor we give Him. Let us bring Him the service gladly and truthfully. He will reward it abundantly.

"The eyes of all wait upon Thee; and Thou givest them their meat in due season." Dear soul, God provides in nature for the creatures He has made. How much more will He provide in grace for those He has redeemed! Learn to say of every want and every failure and every lack of needful grace: I have waited too little upon God, or He would have given me in due season all I needed. And say then, too—

My soul, wait thou only upon God!

Chapter 5

FOR INSTRUCTION

"Show me thy ways, O Lord; Teach me thy paths. Lead me in thy truth, and teach me: For thou art the God of my salvation; On thee do I wait all the day"—Psalm 25:4,5.

I spoke of an army on the point of entering an enemy's territories. Answering the question as to the cause of delay: "Waiting for supplies." The answer might also have been: "Waiting for instructions," or "Waiting for orders." If the last dispatch had not been received, with the final orders of the commander in chief, the army dared not move. It is even so in the Christian life—as deep as the need of *waiting for supplies* is that of *waiting for instructions*.

See how beautifully this comes out in Psalm 25. The writer knew and loved God's laws exceedingly, and he meditated in that law day and night. But, he knew that this was not enough. He knew that for the right spiritual understanding of the truth, and for the right personal application of it to his own particular circumstances, he needed a direct, divine teaching.

The psalm has at all times been a very special one because of its reiterated expression of the felt need of the divine teaching and of the childlike confidence that that teaching would be given. Study the psalm until your heart is filled with the two thoughts—the absolute need and the absolute certainty of divine guidance. And with these, how entirely it is in this connection that he speaks: "On Thee do I wait all the day." Waiting for guidance, waiting for instruction, all the day, is a very blessed part of waiting upon God.

The Father in heaven is so interested in His child, and so longs to have his life at every step in His will and His love, that He is willing to keep his guidance entirely in His own hand. He knows so well that we are unable to do what is really holy and heavenly, except as He works it in us, that He means His very demands to become promises of what He will do, in watching over and leading us all the day. We may count on Him to teach us *His* way, and show us *His* path in special difficulties and times of perplexity, as well as in the common course of everyday life.

And what is necessary for us to receive this guidance? One thing: waiting for instructions, waiting on God. "On Thee do I wait all the day." We want, in our times of prayer, to give clear expression to our sense of need and our faith in His help. We want to definitely become conscious of our ignorance as to what God's way may be. We must be aware of our need of the divine light shining within us, if our way is to be as the sun, shining more and more unto the perfect day. And, we want to wait quietly before God in prayer, until the deep, restful assurance fills us. It will be given—"the meek will He guide in the way."

"On Thee do I wait all the day." The special surrender to the divine guidance in our seasons of prayer must cultivate, and be followed up by, the habitual looking upward "all the day." As simple as it is to walk all day in the light of the sun, so simple and delightful can it become to a soul, practiced in waiting on God, to walk all day in the enjoyment of God's light and leading. What is needed to help us to such a life is just one thing—the real knowledge and faith of God as the only source of wisdom and goodness, as ever ready, and longing much to be to us all that we can possibly require. Yes, this is the one thing we need! If we only saw our God in His love, if we only believed that He waits to be gracious, that He waits to be our life and to work all in us—how this waiting on God would become our highest joy, the natural and spontaneous response of our hearts to His great love and glory!

My soul, wait thou only upon God!

29

Chapter 6

FOR ALL SAINTS

"Let none that wait on thee be ashamed"—Psalm 25:3.

Let us now, each one forgetting himself, think of the great company of God, and the saints throughout the world who are all waiting on Him. And, let us all join in the fervent prayer for each other: "Let none that wait on Thee be ashamed."

Just think for a moment of the many waiting ones who need that prayer, how many are sick and weary and alone, and feel as if their prayers are not answered. They sometimes begin to fear that their hope will be put to shame. And then, think of how many servants of God, ministers or missionaries, teachers or workers, of various name, whose hopes in their work have been disappointed, and whose longing for power and blessing remains unsatisfied. And then, too, think of how many who have heard of a life of rest and perfect peace, of abiding light and fellowship, of strength and victory, and who cannot find the path. With all these, it is only that they have not yet learned the secret of full waiting upon God. They just need what we all need, the living assurance that waiting on God can never be in vain. Let us remember, all who are in danger of fainting or being weary, and unite in the cry, "Let none that wait on Thee be ashamed!"

If this intercession for all who wait on God becomes part of our waiting on Him for ourselves, we will help to bear each other's burdens, and so fulfill the law of Christ.

There will be introduced into our waiting on God that element of unselfishness and love, which is the path to the highest blessing and the fullest communion with God. Love to the brethren and love to God are inseparably linked. In God, the love to His Son *and to us* are one: "That the love wherewith Thou hast loved Me may be in them." In Christ, the love of the Father to Him, and *His love to us*, are one: "As the Father loved Me, so have I loved you." In us, He asks that His love to us be *ours* to the brethren: "As I have loved you, that ye love one another." All the love of God, and of Christ, are inseparably linked with love to the brethren. And how can we, day by day, prove and cultivate this love except by praying daily for each other? Christ did not seek to enjoy the Father's love for Himself; He passed it all on to us. All true seeking of God, and His love for ourselves, will be inseparably linked with the thought and the love of our brethren in prayer for them.

"Let none that wait on Thee be ashamed." Twice

in the psalm David speaks of his waiting on God for himself; here he thinks of *all* who wait on Him. Let this be the message to all God's tried and weary ones, that there are more people praying for them than they know about. Let it stir them and us in our waiting to make a point of at times forgetting ourselves, and to enlarge our hearts and say to the Father: *"These all wait upon Thee,* and Thou givest them their meat in due season." Let it inspire us all with new courage—for who is there who is not at times ready to faint and be weary? "Let none that wait on Thee be ashamed" is a promise in a prayer. "They that wait on Thee shall not be ashamed!" From many a witness, the cry comes to everyone who needs help—brother, sister, tried one, "Wait on the Lord; be of good courage, and He shall strengthen your heart; wait, I say, on the Lord. Be of good courage, and He shall strengthen your heart, all ye that wait on the Lord."

Blessed Father, we humbly beseech You let none who wait on You be ashamed; no, not one. Some are weary, and the time of waiting appears long. And some are feeble and scarcely know how to wait. And some are so entangled in the effort of their prayers and their work, they think that they can find no time to wait continually. Father, teach us all how to wait! Teach us to think of each other, and pray for each other. Teach us to think of You, the God of all waiting ones. Father, let none that wait on You be ashamed! For Jesus' sake. Amen.

My soul, wait thou only upon God!

33

Chapter 7

A PLEA IN PRAYER

"Let integrity and uprightness preserve me; for I wait on thee"—Psalm 25:21.

For the third time in this psalm we have the word *wait*. As before in verse 5, "On Thee do I wait all the day," so here, too, the believing supplicant appeals to God to remember that he is waiting on Him, looking for an answer. It is a great thing for a soul not only to wait upon God, but to be filled with such a consciousness that its whole spirit and position is that of a waiting one. It can, in childlike confidence, say, "Lord, Thou knowest, I wait on Thee!" It will prove a mighty plea in prayer, giving ever-increasing boldness of expectation to claim the promise: "They that wait on Me shall not be ashamed!"

The prayer in connection with which the plea is put forth here is one of great importance in the spiritual life. If we draw near to God, it must be with a true heart. There must be perfect integrity and wholeheartedness in our dealing with God. As we read in the next psalm (26:1,11): "Judge me, O Lord; for I have walked in mine integrity. . . . As for me, I will walk in mine integrity," there must be perfect uprightness of single-heartedness before God, as it is written: "His righteousness is for the upright in heart." The soul must allow nothing sinful, nothing doubtful, if it is indeed to meet the Holy One and receive His full blessing. This can only be done with a heart wholly and singly given up to His will. The whole spirit that animates us in the waiting must be, "Let integrity and uprightness"—You see that I desire to come so to You, You know I am looking to You to work them perfectly in me—let them "preserve me; for I wait on Thee."

And, if at our first attempt truly to live the life of fully and always waiting on God, we begin to discover how much that perfect integrity is wanting, this will just be one of the blessings which the waiting was meant to work. *A soul cannot seek close fellowship with God, or attain the abiding consciousness of waiting on Him all the day, without a very honest and entire surrender to all His will.*

"For I wait on Thee." It is not only in connection with the prayer of our text but with every prayer that this plea may be used. To use it often will be a great blessing to ourselves. Let us, therefore, study the words well until we know all their meanings. It must be clear to us *what we are waiting for*. There may be very different things. It may be waiting for God in our times of prayer to take His place as God, and to work in us the sense of His holy presence and nearness. It may be a special petition to which we are expecting an answer. It may be our whole inner life, in which we are on the lookout for God's putting forth of His power. It may be the whole state of His Church and saints, or some part of His work, for which our eyes are ever toward Him. It is good that we remember and keep track of the things we are waiting for on God. As we say definitely to each of them, "On Thee do I wait," we will be able to claim the answer, *"For* on Thee do I wait."

It must also be clear to us, *on whom we are waiting.* Not an idol, a God of whom we have made an image by our conceptions of what He is. No, but the living God, such as He really is in His great glory, His infinite holiness, His power, wisdom, and goodness, in His love and nearness. It is the presence of a beloved or a dreaded master that awakens the whole attention of the servant who waits on him. It is *the presence of God, as He can in Christ by His Holy Spirit make Himself known,* and keep the soul under its covering and shadow, that will awaken and strengthen the true waiting spirit. Let us be still and wait and worship until we know how near He is, and then say, *"On Thee* do I wait."

And then, let it be very clear, too, that *we are waiting.* Let that become so much our consciousness that the utterance comes spontaneously, "On Thee *I do wait* all the day; *I wait* on Thee." This will indeed imply sacrifice and separation, a soul entirely given up to God as its all, its only joy. This waiting on God has hardly been acknowledged as the only true

Christianity. And yet, if it is true that God alone is goodness and joy and love, if it is true that our highest blessedness is in having as much of God as we can, if it is true that Christ has redeemed us wholly for God and made a life of continual abiding in His presence possible, nothing less ought to satisfy us than to be ever breathing this blessed atmosphere, "I wait on Thee."

My soul, wait thou only upon God!

Chapter 8

STRONG AND OF GOOD COURAGE

"Wait on the Lord: be strong, And let thine heart take courage; Yea, wait thou on the Lord"—Psalm 27:14 (Eng. Rev.).

The Psalmist has just said: "I had fainted, unless I had believed to see the goodness of the Lord in the land of the living." If it had not been for his faith in God, his heart would have fainted. But, in the confident assurance in God which faith gives, he urges himself and us to remember one thing above all—to wait upon God. "Wait on the Lord: be strong, and let your heart take courage: yea, wait thou on the Lord." One of the chief needs in our waiting upon God, one of the deepest secrets of its blessedness and blessing, is a quiet, confident persuasion that it is not in vain. Have courage and believe that God will hear and help. We are waiting on a God who could never disappoint His people.

"Be strong and of good courage." These words are frequently found in connection with some great and difficult enterprise, in prospect of the combat with the power of strong enemies, and the utter insufficiency of all human strength. Is waiting on God a work so difficult, that such words are needed: "Be strong, and let your heart take courage"? Yes, indeed. The deliverance for which we often have to wait is from enemies, in whose presence we are so weak. The blessings for which we plead are spiritual and all unseen—things impossible with men—heavenly, supernatural, divine realities. Our heart may well faint and fail.

Our souls are so little accustomed to hold fellowship with God, the God on whom we wait so often *appears* to hide Himself. We who have to wait are often tempted to fear that we do not wait enough, that our faith is too feeble, that our desire is not as upright or as earnest as it should be, that our surrender is not complete. Amid all these causes of fear or doubt, how blessed to hear the voice of God: "Wait on the Lord! Be strong, and let thine heart take courage! Yea, wait thou on the Lord!" Let nothing in heaven or earth or hell keep you from waiting on your God in full assurance that it cannot be in vain.

The one lesson our text teaches us is this, that when we set ourselves to wait on God we ought, beforehand, to resolve that it will be with the most confident expectation of God's meeting and blessing us. We ought to make up our minds to this, that nothing was ever so sure as that waiting on God will bring us untold and unexpected blessing. We are so accustomed to judge the work of God in us by *what we feel,* that the great probability is that when we begin to cultivate the waiting on Him, we will be discouraged because we do not find any special blessing from it. The message comes to us: "Above everything, when you wait on God, do so in the spirit of abounding hopefulness. It is God in His glory, in His power, in His love longing to bless you that you are waiting on."

If you say that you are afraid of deceiving yourself with vain hope, because you do not see or feel any evidence in your present state for such special expectations, my answer is, It is God who is the reason for your expecting great things. Oh, do learn the lesson! You are not going to wait on yourself to see what you feel and what changes come to you. You are going to *wait on God,* to know *first what He is,* and then after that, what He will do. The whole duty and blessedness of waiting on God has its roots in this, that He is such a blessed Being, full, to overflowing, of goodness and power and life and joy, that we, however wretched, cannot for any time come into contact with Him without that life and power secretly, silently beginning to enter into us and blessing us. God is love! That is the only and all-sufficient warrant of your expectation. Love seeketh not its own. God's love is just *His delight to impart Himself and His blessedness* to His children.

Come, and however feeble you feel, just wait in His presence. As a feeble, sickly invalid is brought out into the sunshine to let its warmth go through him, come with all that is dark and cold in you *into the sunshine of God's holy, omnipotent love*. Sit and wait there, with the one thought: Here I am, in the sunshine of His love. As the sun does its work in the weak one who seeks its rays, *God will do His work in you*. Oh, do trust Him fully! "Wait on the Lord! Be strong, and let your heart take courage! Yea, wait thou on the Lord!"

My soul, wait thou only upon God!

Chapter 9

WITH THE HEART

"Be strong, and let your heart take courage, All ye that wait for the Lord"—Psalm 31:24 (Eng. Rev.).

The words are nearly the same as in our last meditation. But, I gladly avail myself of them again to stress a much-needed lesson for all who desire to truly and fully learn what waiting on God is. The lesson is this: It is *with the heart* that we must wait upon God. "Let *your heart* take courage." All our waiting depends on the state of the heart. As a man's heart is, so is he before God. We can advance no further or deeper into the holy place of God's presence to wait on Him there, than our heart is prepared for it by the Holy Spirit. The message is: *"Let your heart* take courage, all ye that wait on the Lord."

The truth appears so simple that some may ask, Do not all admit this? Where is the need of insisting on it so specially? Because very many Christians have no sense of the great difference between the Christianity of the mind and the Christianity of the

heart, and the former is far more diligently cultivated than the latter. They do not know how infinitely greater the heart is than the mind. It is this that
causes much of the feebleness of our Christian life.
And, it is only as this is understood that waiting on
God will bring its full blessing.

Proverbs 3:5 may help to make my meaning clear.
Speaking of a life in the fear and favor of God, it
says: "Trust in the Lord with all thine heart; and lean
not unto thine own understanding." In all faith, we
have to use these two powers. The mind has to
gather knowledge from God's Word, and prepare
the food by which the heart with the inner life is to be
nourished. But, here is the terrible danger of our
leaning to our own understanding, and trusting in
our own comprehension of divine things.

People imagine that if they are occupied with the
truth, the spiritual life will, as a matter of course, be
strengthened. And, this is by no means the case. The
understanding deals with conceptions and images of
divine things, but it cannot reach the real life of the
soul. Hence the command: "Trust in the Lord with
all thine heart, and lean not upon thine own understanding." It is with the heart that man believes and
comes into touch with God. It is in the heart that
God has given His Spirit to be the presence and the
power of God working in us. In all our faith, it is the
heart that must trust and love and worship and obey.
My mind is utterly unable to create or maintain the
spiritual life within me. The heart must wait on God
for Him to work it in me.

It is in this even as in the physical life. My reason may tell me what to eat and drink, and how the food nourishes me. But, in the eating and feeding my reasons can do nothing—the body has its organs for that special purpose. Just so, reason may tell me what God's Word says, but it can do nothing to the feeding of the soul on the bread of life—this the heart alone can do by its faith and trust in God. A man may be studying the nature and effects of food or sleep. When he wants to eat or sleep he sets aside his thoughts and study, and uses the power of eating or sleeping. And so, the Christian always needs, when he has studied or heard God's Word, to cease from his thoughts, to put no trust in them, to awaken his heart to open itself before God, and seek the living fellowship with Him.

This is now the blessedness of waiting upon God: that I confess the utter weakness of all my thoughts and efforts, and set myself still to bow my heart before Him in holy silence, and to trust Him to renew and strengthen His own work in me. And, this is just the lesson of our text: "Let *your heart* take courage, all ye that wait on the Lord." Remember the difference between knowing with the mind and believing with the heart. Beware of the temptation of leaning upon your understanding, with its clear strong thoughts. They only help you to know what the heart must get from God—in themselves they are only images and shadows.

"Let *your heart* take courage, all ye that wait on the Lord." Present it before Him as that wonderful part of your spiritual nature in which God reveals Himself, and by which you can know Him. Cultivate the greatest confidence that though you cannot see into your heart, God is working there by His Holy Spirit. Let the heart wait at times in perfect silence and quiet; in its hidden depths God will work. Be sure of this, and just wait on Him. Give your whole heart, with its secret workings, into God's hands continually. He wants the heart. He takes it, and, as God, dwells in it. "Be strong, and let your heart take courage, all ye that wait on the Lord."

My soul, wait thou only upon God!

Chapter 10

IN HUMBLE FEAR AND HOPE

"Behold, the eye of the Lord is upon them that fear him, Upon them that hope in his mercy; To deliver their soul from death, And to keep them alive in famine. Our soul hath waited for the Lord: He is our help and our shield. For our heart shall rejoice in him, Because we have trusted in his holy name. Let thy mercy, O Lord, be upon us, According as we wait for thee"—Psalm 33:18-22 (Eng. Rev.).

God's eye is upon His people; their eye is upon Him. In waiting upon God, our eye, looking up to Him, meets His looking down upon us. This is the blessedness of waiting upon God, that it takes our eyes and thoughts away from ourselves, even our needs and desires, and occupies us with our God. We worship Him in His glory and love, with His all-seeing eye watching over us, that He may supply our every need. Let us consider this wonderful meeting between God and His people, and notice what we are taught here of them on whom God's eye rests, and of

Him on whom our eye rests.

"The eye of the Lord is on them that *fear* Him, on them that *hope* in His mercy." Fear and hope are generally thought to be in conflict with each other. In the presence and worship of God, they are found side by side in perfect and beautiful harmony. And this, because in God Himself all apparent contradictions are reconciled. Righteousness and peace, judgment and mercy, holiness and love, infinite power and infinite gentleness, a majesty that is exalted above all heaven, and a condescension that bows very low, meet and kiss each other.

There is indeed a fear that has torment, that is cast out entirely by perfect love. But, there is a fear that is found in the very heavens. In the song of Moses and the Lamb they sing: "Who shall not fear Thee, O Lord, and glorify Thy name?" And out of the very throne the voice came: "Praise our God, all ye His servants, and ye that fear Him." Let us in our waiting ever seek "to fear the glorious and fearful name, the Lord thy God." The deeper we bow before His holiness in holy fear and adoring awe, in deep reverence and humble self-abasement, even as the angels veil their faces before the throne, the more His holiness will rest upon us. Then, we will be filled to have God reveal Himself. The deeper we enter into the truth "that no flesh glory in His presence," will it be given us to see His glory. "The eye of the Lord is on them that fear Him."

"On them that hope in His mercy." So far will the true fear of God be from keeping us back from hope, it will stimulate and strengthen it. The lower we bow, the deeper we feel we have nothing to hope in but His mercy. The lower we bow, the nearer God will come and make our hearts bold to trust Him. Let every exercise of waiting, let our whole habit of waiting on God, be pervaded by abounding hope—a hope as bright and boundless as God's mercy. The fatherly kindness of God is such that, in whatever state we come to Him, we may confidently hope in His mercy.

Such are God's waiting ones. And now, think of the God on whom we wait. "The eye of the Lord is on them that fear Him, on them that hope in His mercy; to deliver their soul from death, and to keep them alive in famine." Not to prevent the danger of death and famine—this is often needed to stir the waiting on Him—but to deliver and keep alive. For the dangers are often very real and dark; the situation, whether in the temporal or spiritual life, may appear to be utterly hopeless. There is always one hope: *God's eye is on them.*

That eye sees the danger, sees in tender love His trembling waiting child, sees the moment when the heart is ripe for the blessing, and sees the way in which it is to come. This living, mighty God, oh, let us fear Him and hope in His mercy! And, let us humbly but boldly say: "Our soul waiteth for the Lord; He is our help and our shield. Let Thy mercy be upon us, O Lord, according as we wait for Thee."

Oh, the blessedness of waiting on such a God! A very present help in every time of trouble; a shield and defense against every danger. Children of God, will you not learn to sink down in entire helplessness and inability, and in stillness to wait and see the salvation of God! In the utmost spiritual famine, and when death appears to prevail, oh, wait on God! He does deliver; He does keep alive. Say it not only in solitude, but say it to each other—the psalm speaks not of one but of God's people—*"Our* soul waiteth on the Lord: He is *our* help and *our* shield." Strengthen and encourage each other in the holy exercise of waiting, that each may not only say of himself, but of his brethren, *"We* have waited for Him; *we* will be glad and rejoice in His salvation."

My soul, wait thou only upon God!

Chapter 11

PATIENTLY

*"Rest in the Lord, and wait patiently for him
....Those that wait upon the Lord, they shall
inherit the land"*—Psalm 37:7,9 (Eng. Rev.).

"In patience possess your souls." "Ye have need of
patience." "Let patience have its perfect work, that
ye may be perfect and entire." Such words of the
Holy Spirit show us what an important element, in
the Christian life and character, patience is. And,
nowhere is there a better place for cultivating or
displaying it than in waiting on God. There, we
discover how impatient we are and what our impa-
tience means. We confess, at times, that we are
impatient with men and circumstances which hinder
us, or with ourselves and our slow progress in the
Christian life. If we truly set ourselves to wait upon
God, we will find that it is with Him we are impatient, because He does not at once, or as soon as we
would wish, do our bidding. It is in waiting upon
God that our eyes are opened to believe in His wise

and sovereign will. Then, we will see that the sooner and the more completely we absolutely yield to it, the more surely His blessing can come to us.

"It is not of him that willeth, nor of him that runneth, but of God that showeth mercy." We have as little power to increase or strengthen our spiritual life as we had to originate it. We "were born not of the will of the flesh, nor of the will of man, but of the will of God." Even so, our willing and running, our desire and effort, avail nothing; all is "of God that showeth mercy."

All the exercises of the spiritual life, our reading and praying, our willing and doing, have their value. But, they can go no farther than this, that they point the way and prepare us in humility to look to and depend upon God Himself, and in patience to wait His good time and mercy. The waiting is to teach us our absolute dependence upon God's mighty working, and to make us, in perfect patience, place ourselves at His disposal. They that wait on the Lord will inherit the land; the promised land and its blessing. The heirs must wait; they can afford to wait.

"Rest in the Lord, and wait patiently for Him." The margin gives for "Rest in the Lord," "Be silent to the Lord," or "Be still before the Lord" (A.S.V.). It is resting in the Lord, in His will, His promise, His faithfulness, and His love, that makes patience easy. And, the resting in Him is nothing but being silent unto Him, still before Him. Having our thoughts and wishes, our fears and hopes, hushed into calm and quiet in that great peace of God which passes all understanding. That peace keeps the heart and mind when we are anxious for anything, because we have made our request known to Him. The rest, the silence, the stillness, and the patient waiting, all find their strength and joy in God Himself.

The need for patience, and the reasonableness and the blessedness of patience will be disclosed to the waiting soul. Our patience will be seen to be the counterpart of God's patience. He longs far more to bless us fully than we can desire it. But, as the husbandman has long patience until the fruit ripens, so God bows Himself to our slowness and bears long with us. Let us remember this, and wait patiently. Of each promise and every answer to prayer the word is true: "I the Lord will hasten it *in its time.*"

"Rest in the Lord, and wait patiently for Him." Yes, *for* Him. Seek not only the help, the gift, seek Himself; wait for Him. Give God His glory by resting in Him, by trusting Him fully, by waiting patiently for Him. This patience honors Him greatly. It leaves Him, as God on the throne, to do His work. It yields self wholly into His hands. It lets God *be God*. If your waiting is for some special request, wait patiently. If your waiting is more an exercise of the spiritual life seeking to know and have more of God, wait patiently. Whether it is in the shorter specific periods of waiting, or as the continuous habit of the soul, rest in the Lord, be still before the Lord, and wait patiently. "They that wait on the Lord shall inherit the land."

My soul, wait thou only upon God!

Chapter 12

KEEPING HIS WAYS

"Wait on the Lord, and keep his way, And he shall exalt thee to inherit the land"—Psalm 37:34.

If we desire to find a man whom we long to meet, we inquire as to the places in which he is to be found. When waiting on God, we need to be very careful that we keep His ways; outside of these we never can expect to find Him. "Thou meetest him that rejoiceth and worketh righteousness; those that remember *Thee in Thy ways.*" We may be sure that God is never and nowhere to be found but in His way. There, by the soul who seeks and patiently waits, He is always most surely to be found. "Wait on the Lord, and keep His way, and He shall exalt thee."

How close is the connection between the two parts of the injunction, "Wait on the Lord"—which has to do with worship and disposition—"and keep His way"—which deals with walk and work. The outer life must be in harmony with the inner; the inner must be the inspiration and the strength for the

55

outer. It is our God who has made His way known in His Word for our conduct, and invites our confidence for His grace and help in our heart. If we do not keep His way, our waiting on Him can bring no blessing. The surrender to a full obedience to all His will is the secret of full access to all the blessings of His fellowship.

Notice how strongly this comes out in the psalm. It speaks of the evil doer who prospers in his way, and calls on the believer not to worry himself. When we see men around us prosperous and happy while they forsake God's ways, and ourselves left in difficulty or suffering, we are in danger of first fretting at what appears so strange, and then gradually yielding to seek our prosperity in their path. The psalm says: "Fret not thyself.... Trust in the Lord, and do good.... Rest in the Lord, and wait patiently for Him.... Cease from anger, and forsake wrath .... Depart from evil, and do good.... The Lord ...forsaketh not His saints.... The righteous shall inherit the land.... The law of his God is in his heart; none of his steps shall slide." And then follows—the word occurs for the third time in the psalm—*"Wait* on the Lord, *and keep His way."* Do what God asks you to do; God will do more than you can ask Him to do.

And, let no one give way to the fear: I cannot keep His way. It is this that robs believers of every confidence. It is true you have not the strength yet to keep His way. But, carefully keep those for which you have received strength already. Surrender yourself willingly and trustingly to keep all God's ways, in the strength which will come in waiting on Him. Give up your whole being to God without reserve and without doubt. He will prove Himself God to you, and work in you that which is pleasing in His sight through Jesus Christ.

Keep His ways as you know them in the Word. Keep His ways, as nature teaches them, in always doing what appears right. Keep His ways as providence points them out. Keep His ways as the Holy Spirit suggests. Do not think of waiting on God while you say you are not willing to work in His path. However weak you feel, only be willing, and He who has worked to will, will work to *do* by His power.

"Wait on the Lord, and keep His way." It may be that the consciousness of shortcoming and sin makes our text look more like a hindrance than a help in waiting on God. Let it not be so. Have we not said more than once that the very starting point and groundwork of this waiting is utter and absolute weakness? Why then do you not come with everything evil you feel in yourself, every memory of unwillingness, unwatchfulness, unfaithfulness, and all that causes such unceasing self-condemnation? Put your power in God's omnipotence, and find your deliverance in waiting on God.

Your failure has been due to only one thing. You sought to conquer and obey in your own strength. Come and bow before God until you learn that He is the God who alone is good, and alone can work any good thing. Believe that in you, and all that nature can do, there is no true power. Be content to receive from God each moment the inworking of His mighty grace and life. Then, waiting on God will become the renewal of your strength to run in His ways and not be weary, to walk in His paths and never faint. "Wait on the Lord, and keep His way" will be command and promise in one.

My soul, wait thou only upon God!

29/5

Chapter 13

FOR MORE THAN WE KNOW

"And now, Lord, what wait I for? My hope is in thee. Deliver me from all my transgressions"—Psalm 39:7,8.

There may be times when we feel as if we do not know what we are waiting for. There may be other times when we think we do know, and when it would be good for us to realize that we do not know how to ask as we ought. God is able to do for us exceeding abundantly above what we ask or think. And, we are in danger of limiting Him when we confine our desires and prayers to our own thoughts of them. It is a great thing at times to say, as our psalm says: "And now, Lord, what wait I for?" I scarcely know or can tell; this only I can say—"My hope is in Thee."

How we see this limiting of God in the case of Israel! When Moses promised them meat in the wilderness, they doubted, saying: "Can God furnish a table in the wilderness? He smote the rock that the water gushed out; can He give bread also? Can He provide flesh for His people?" If they had been asked whether God could provide streams in the desert, they would have answered, Yes. God had done it; He could do it again. But, when they thought of God doing something new, they limited Him. Their expectation could not rise beyond their past experience, or their own thoughts of what was possible.

Even so, we may be limiting God by our conceptions of what He has promised or is able to do. Do let us beware of limiting the Holy One of Israel in our prayer. Let us believe that the very promises of God we plead have a divine meaning, infinitely beyond our thoughts of them. Let us believe that His fulfillment of them can be, in a power and an abundance of grace, beyond our largest grasping of thought. And, let us, therefore, cultivate the habit of waiting on God, not only for what we think we need, but for all that His grace and power are ready to do for us.

In every true prayer, there are two hearts in exercise. The one is your heart, with its little, dark, human thoughts of what you need and God can do. The other is God's great heart, with its infinite, its divine purposes of blessing. What think you? To which of these two ought the larger place be given in your approach to Him? Undoubtedly, to the heart of God. Everything depends upon knowing and being occupied with that. But, how little this is done. This is what waiting on God is meant to teach you. Just think of God's wonderful love and redemption, in the meaning these words must have to Him. Confess how little you understand what God is willing to do for you, and say each time as you pray: "And now, Lord, what wait I for?" My heart cannot say. God's heart knows and waits to give. "My hope is in Thee." Wait on God to do more for you than you can ask or think.

Apply this to the prayer that follows: "Deliver me from all my transgressions." You have prayed to be delivered from temper or pride or self-will. It is as if it is in vain. May it not be that you have had your own thoughts about the way or the extent of God's doing it, and have never waited on the God of glory, according to the riches of His glory, to do for you what the hearts of man cannot conceive?

Learn to worship God as the God who does wonders, who wishes to prove in you that He can do something supernatural and divine. Bow before Him, wait upon Him, until your soul realizes that you are in the hands of a divine and almighty worker. Consent but to know what and how He will work. Expect it to be something altogether godlike, something to be waited for in deep humility, and received only by His divine power. Let the "And now, Lord, what wait I for? My hope is in Thee" become the spirit of every longing and every prayer. He will, in His time, do His work.

Dear soul, in waiting on God you may often be weary, because you hardly know what to expect. I pray you, be of good courage—this ignorance is often one of the best signs. He is teaching you to leave all in His hands, and to wait on Him alone.

"Wait on the Lord! Be strong, and let your heart take courage. Yea, wait thou on the Lord."

My soul, wait thou only upon God!

Chapter 14

THE WAY TO THE NEW SONG

"I waited patiently for the Lord; and he inclined unto me, and heard my cry....And he hath put a new song in my mouth, even praise unto our God"—Psalm 40:1,3.

Come and listen to the testimony of one who can speak from experience of the sure and blessed outcome of patient waiting upon God. True patience is so foreign to our self-confident nature, it is so indispensable in our waiting upon God, it is such an essential element of true faith, that we would do well to once again meditate on what the Word has to teach us.

The word patience is derived from the Latin word for suffering. It suggests the thought of being under the constraint of some power from which we would gladly be free. At first, we submit against our will. Experience teaches us that when it is vain to resist, patient endurance is our wisest course. In waiting on God, it is of infinite consequence that we not only submit, because we are compelled to, but because we lovingly and joyfully consent to be in the hands of our blessed Father. Patience then becomes our highest blessedness and our highest grace. It honors God, and gives Him time to have His way with us. It is the highest expression of our faith in His goodness and faithfulness. It brings the soul perfect rest in the assurance that God is carrying on His work. It is the token of our full consent that God should deal with us in such a way and time as He thinks best. True patience is the losing of our self-will in His perfect will.

Such patience is needed for the true and full waiting on God. Such patience is the growth and fruit of our first lesson in the school of waiting. To many, it will appear strange how difficult it is to truly wait upon God. The great stillness of soul before God that sinks into its own helplessness and waits for Him to reveal Himself must be waited for. The deep humility that is afraid to let its own will or own strength work except as God works to will and to do requires patience. The meekness that is content to be and to know nothing except as God gives His light takes time. The entire resignation of the will that only wants to be a vessel in which His holy will can move and mold is not found at once. But, each will come in measure as the soul maintains its position, and continually says: "Truly my soul waiteth upon God; from Him cometh my salvation: He only is my rock and my salvation."

Have you ever noticed what proof we have that

patience is a grace for which very special grace is given? Notice these words of Paul: *"Stengthened with all might, according to His glorious power, unto all"*—what? *"patience and long-suffering with joyfulness."* Yes, we need to be strengthened with all God's might, according to the measure of His glorious power, if we are to wait on God in all patience. It is God revealing Himself in us as our life and strength that will enable us, with perfect patience, to leave all in His hands. If any are inclined to despond, because they do not have such patience, let them be of good courage. It is in the course of our feeble and very imperfect waiting that God Himself, by His hidden power, strengthens us and works out in us the patience of the saints, the patience of Christ Himself.

Listen to the voice of one who was deeply tried: "I waited patiently for the Lord; and He inclined unto me, and heard my cry." Hear what he passed through: "He brought me up also out of an horrible pit, out of the miry clay, and set my feet upon a rock, and established my goings. And He hath put a new song in my mouth, even praise unto our God." Patient waiting upon God brings a rich reward; the deliverance is sure. God Himself will put a new song into your mouth. O soul, do not be impatient, whether it is in the exercise of prayer and worship that you find it difficult to wait, in the delay of definite requests, or in the fulfillment of your heart's desire for the revelation of God Himself in a deeper spiritual life! Fear not, but rest in the Lord, and wait patiently for Him.

- And, if you sometimes feel as if patience is not your gift, them remember *it is* God's gift, and take that prayer (2 Thessalonians 3:5, A.S.V.): "The Lord directs your hearts into the...patience of Christ." Into the patience with which you are to wait on God, He Himself will guide you.

My soul, wait thou only upon God!

Chapter 15

FOR HIS COUNSEL

"They soon forgat his works: they waited not for his counsel"—Psalm 106:13.

This refers to the sin of God's people in the wilderness. He had wonderfully redeemed them, and was prepared to just as wonderfully supply their every need. But, when the time of need came, "they waited not for His counsel." They did not think that the Almighty God was their Leader and Provider. They did not ask what His plans might be. They simply thought the thoughts of their own hearts, and tempted and provoked God by their unbelief. "They waited not for His counsel."

How this has been the sin of God's people in all ages! In the land of Canaan, in the days of Joshua, the only three failures of which we read were owing to this one sin. In going up against Ai, in making a covenant with the Gibeonites, in settling down without going up to possess the whole land, they waited not for His counsel. And so, even the advanced believer is in danger from this most subtle of temptations—taking God's Word, thinking his own thoughts of them, and not waiting for His counsel. Let us heed the warning and see what Israel teaches us. And, let us very specially regard it not only as a danger to which the individual is exposed, but as one against which God's people, in their collective capacity, need to be on their guard.

Our whole relationship to God is ruled in this, that His will is to be done in us and by us as it is in heaven. He has promised to make known His will to us by His Spirit, the Guide into all truth. And, our position is to be that of waiting for His counsel as the only guide of our thoughts and actions. In our church worship, in our prayer meetings, in our conventions, in all our gatherings as managers or directors or committees or helpers in any part of the work for God, our first object must always be to ascertain the mind of God. God always works according to the counsel of His will. The more that counsel of His will is sought and found and honored, the more surely and mightily will God do His work for us and through us.

The great danger in all such assemblies is that in our consciousness of having our Bible, in our past experience of God's leading, in our sound creed and our honest wish to do God's will, we trust in these and do not realize that with every step we need and may have a heavenly guidance. There may be elements of God's will, application of God's Word, experience of the close presence and leading of God, manifestations of the power of His Spirit, of which we know nothing as yet. God may be willing, no, God *is* willing to open up these to the souls who are intently set upon allowing Him to have His way entirely, and who are willing, in patience, to wait for Him to make it known.

When we come together praising God for all He has done and taught and given, we may, at the same time, be limiting Him by not expecting greater things. It was when God had given the water out of the rock that they did not trust Him for bread. It was when God had given Jericho into his hands that Joshua thought the victory over Ai was sure, and did not wait for counsel from God. And so, while we think that we know and trust the power of God for what we may expect, we may be hindering Him by not giving Him time, and not definitely cultivating the habit of waiting for His counsel.

A minister has no more solemn duty than to teach people to wait upon God. Why was it that in the house of Cornelius, when "Peter spake these words, the Holy Ghost fell upon all that heard him"? They had said: "We are here *before* God to hear all things that are commanded thee *of God."* We may come together to give and to listen to the most earnest exposition of God's truth with little spiritual profit if there is no waiting for God's counsel.

And so, in all our gatherings we need to believe in the Holy Spirit as the Guide and Teacher of God's saints. They must wait to be led by Him into the things which God has prepared, and which the heart cannot conceive.

More stillness of soul to realize God's presence; more consciousness of ignorance of what God's great plans may be; more faith in the certainty that God has greater things to show us; that He Himself will be revealed in new glory—these must be the marks of the assemblies of God's saints if they would avoid the reproach: "They waited not for His counsel."

My soul, wait thou only upon God!

Chapter 16

AND HIS LIGHT IN THE HEART

"I wait for the Lord, my soul doth wait, And in his word do I hope. My soul waiteth for the Lord more than they that watch for the morning: I say, more than they that watch for the morning"—Psalm 130:5,6.

How intensely the morning light is often waited for. By the mariners in a shipwrecked vessel; by a benighted traveler in a dangerous country; by an army which finds itself surrounded by an enemy. The morning light will show what hope of escape there may be. The morning may bring life and liberty. And so, the saints of God in darkness have longed for the light of His countenance, more than watchmen for the morning. They have said: "More than watchmen for the morning, my soul waiteth for the Lord." Can we say that, too? Our waiting on God can have no higher object than simply having His light shine on us, in us, and through us, all day.

God is light. God is a sun. Paul says: "God hath

shined in our hearts to give the light." What light? "The light of the glory of God, in the face of Jesus Christ." Just as the sun shines its beautiful, life-giving light on and into our earth, so God shines into our hearts the light of His glory, of His love, in Christ His Son. Our heart is meant to have that light filling and gladdening it all day. It can have it because God is our sun, and it is written, "Thy sun shall no more go down forever." God's love shines on us without ceasing.

But, can we indeed enjoy it all day? We can. And how can we? Let nature give us the answer. Those beautiful trees and flowers, with all this green grass, what do they do to keep the sun shining on them? They do nothing; they simply bask in the sunshine, when it comes. The sun is millions of miles away, but over all that distance it comes, its own light and joy. And, the tiniest flower that lifts its little head upward is met by the same exuberance of light and blessing as flood the widest landscape. We do not have to care for the light we need for our day's work. The sun cares, and provides and shines the light around us all day. We simply count upon it, receive it, and enjoy it.

The only difference between nature and grace is this, that what the trees and the flowers do unconsciously, as they drink in the blessing of the light, is to be, for us, a voluntary and loving acceptance. Faith, simple faith in God's Word and love, is to be the opening of the eyes and the heart, to receive and enjoy the unspeakable glory of His grace. And just

72

as the trees, day by day and month by month, stand and grow into beauty and fruitfulness, just welcoming whatever sunshine the sun may give, so it is the very highest exercise of our Christian life just to abide in the light of God. Let it, and let Him, fill us with the life and the brightness it brings.

And if you ask, But can it really be, that just as naturally and heartily as I recognize and rejoice in the beauty of a bright sunny morning, I can rejoice in God's light all day? It can, indeed. From my breakfast table I look out on a beautiful valley, with trees and vineyards and mountains. In our spring and autumn months, the light in the morning is exquisite, and almost involunatirly we say, How beautiful! And the question comes, Is it only the light of the sun that is to bring such continual beauty and joy? And is there no provision for the light of God being just as much an unceasing source of joy and gladness? There is, indeed, if the soul will only be still and wait on Him. Only let God shine.

Dear soul, learn to wait on the Lord, more than watchers for the morning! All within you may be very dark. But, is that not the very best reason for waiting for the light of God? The beginnings of light may be just enough to discover the darkness, and painfully to humble you on account of sin. Can you not trust the light to expel the darkness? Do believe it will. Just bow, even now, in stillness before God, and wait on Him to shine into you. Say, in humble faith, God is light, infinitely brighter and more beautiful than that of the sun. God is light—the Father.

The eternal, inaccessible, and incomprehensible light—the Son. The light concentrated, embodied, and manifested—the Spirit, the light entering and dwelling and shining in our hearts. God is light, and is here shining on my heart. I have been so occupied with the rushlights of my thoughts and efforts that I have never opened the shutters to let His light in. Unbelief has kept it out.

I bow in faith—God, light, is shining into my heart. The God of whom Paul wrote: "God hath shined into our heart," is my God. What would I think of a sun that could not shine? What would I think of a God who does not shine? No, God shines! God is light! I will take time, just be still, and rest in the light of God. My eyes are feeble, and the windows are not clean, but I will wait on the Lord. The light does shine, the light will shine in me, and make me full of light. And, I will learn to walk all day in the light and joy of God. My soul waits on the light of the Lord, more than the watchers for the morning.

My soul, wait thou only upon God!

Chapter 17

IN TIMES OF DARKNESS

"I will wait upon the Lord, that hideth his face from the house of Jacob, and I will look for him"—Isaiah 8:17.

Here we have a servant of God waiting upon Him, not on behalf of himself, but of his people, from whom God was hiding His face. It suggests to us how our waiting upon God, though it commences with our personal needs, with the desire for the revelation of Himself, or of the answer to personal petitions, need not, may not, stop there. We may be walking in the full light of God's countenance, and yet God may be hiding His face from His people around us. Far from our being content to think that this is nothing but the just punishment of their sin, or the consequence of their indifference, we are called with tender hearts to think of their sad estate, and to wait on God on their behalf. The privilege of waiting upon God is one that brings great responsibility. Even as Christ, when He entered God's presence, at once used His place of privilege and honor as intercessor, so we, no less, if we know what it is to really enter in and wait upon God, must use our access for our less favored brethren. "I will wait upon the Lord, who hideth His face from the house of Jacob."

You worship with a certain congregation. Possibly, there is not the spiritual life or joy either in the preaching or in the fellowship that you desire. You belong to a church with its many services. There is so much error or worldliness, so much seeking after human wisdom and culture, or so much trust in ordinances and observances, that you are not surprised that God hides His face in many cases. It is no wonder that there is little power for conversion or true edification.

Then, there are branches of Christian work with which you are connected—a Sunday school, a Gospel hall, a young men's association, a mission work abroad—in which the feebleness of the Spirit's working appears to indicate that God is hiding His face. You think, too, you know the reason. There is too much trust in men and money. There is too much formality and self-indulgence. There is too little faith and prayer; too little love and humility; too little of the spirit of the crucified Jesus. At times, you feel as if things are hopeless, and that nothing will help.

Do believe that God can and will help. Let the spirit of the prophet come into you, as you value his words, and set yourself to wait on God, on behalf of His erring children. Instead of the tone of judgment

76

or condemnation, of despondency or despair, realize your calling to wait upon God. If others fail in doing it, give yourself doubly to it. The deeper the darkness, the greater the need of appealing to the only Deliverer. The greater the self-confidence around you, that knows not that it is poor and wretched and blind, the more urgent the call to be at your post waiting upon God. Say on each new occasion, when you are tempted to speak or to sigh: "I will wait on the Lord, who hideth His face from the house of Jacob."

There is a still larger circle—the Christian Church throughout the world. Think of Greek, Roman Catholic, and Protestant churches, and the state of the millions who belong to them. Or, think only of the Protestant churches with their open Bible and orthodox creeds. How much nominal profession and formality! How much of the rule of the flesh and of man in the very temple of God! And, what abundant proof that God does hide His face!

What are those who see and mourn this to do? The first thing to be done is this: "I will wait on the Lord, who hideth His face from the house of Jacob." Let us wait on God, in the humble confession of the sins of His people. Let us take time and wait on Him in this exercise. Let us wait on God in tender, loving intercession for all saints, our beloved brethren, however wrong their lives or their teaching may appear. Let us wait on God in faith and expectation, until He shows us that He will hear. Let us wait on God, with the simple offering of ourselves to Himself, and the earnest prayer that He would send us to our brethren. Let us wait on God, and give Him no rest until He makes Zion a joy in the earth.

Yes, let us rest in the Lord, and wait patiently for Him who now hides His face from so many of His children. And, let us say of the lifting up of the light of His countenance we long for all His people, "I wait for the Lord, my soul doth wait, and my hope is in His word. My soul waiteth for the Lord, more than the watchers for the morning, the watchers for the morning."

My soul, wait thou only upon God!

Chapter 18

TO REVEAL HIMSELF

"And it shall be said in that day, Lo, this is our God; we have waited for him, and he will save us: this is the Lord; we have waited for him, we will be glad and rejoice in his salvation"—Isaiah 25:9.

In this passage, we have two precious thoughts. The one, that it is the language of God's people who have been unitedly waiting on Him. The other, that the fruit of their waiting has been that God has so revealed Himself, that they could joyfully say: "Lo, this is our God...this is the Lord." The power and the blessing of united waiting is what we need to learn.

Note that this phrase is repeated twice, "We have waited for Him." In some time of trouble, the hearts of the people had been drawn together, and they had, ceasing from all human hope or help, with one heart set themselves to wait for their God. Is this not just what we need in our churches and conventions and prayer meetings? Is not the need of the Church, and the world great enough to demand it? Are there not in the Church of Christ evils to which no human wisdom is equal? Have we not ritualism and rationalism, formalism and worldliness, robbing the Church of its power? Have we not culture and money and pleasure threatening its spiritual life? Are not the powers of the Church utterly inadequate to cope with the powers of infidelity and iniquity and wretchedness in Christian countries and in heathendom? And, is there not, in the promise of God and in the power of the Holy Spirit, a provision made that can meet the need, and give the Church the restful assurance that she is doing all her God expects of her? And, would not united waiting upon God for the supply of His Spirit most certainly seem the needed blessing? We cannot doubt it.

The object of a more definite waiting upon God in our gatherings would be very much the same as in personal worship. It would mean a deeper conviction that God must and will do all. It would require a more humble and abiding entrance into our deep helplessness, and the need of entire and unceasing dependence upon Him. We need a more living consciousness that the essential thing is to give God His place of honor and of power. We must have a confident expectation that to those who wait on Him, God will, by His Spirit, give the secret of His acceptance and presence, and then, in due time, the revelation of His saving power. The great aim would be to bring everyone in a praying and worshipping company under a deep sense of God's presence, so that when they part there will be the consciousness of having met God Himself, of having left every request with Him, and of now waiting in stillness while He works out His salvation.

It is this experience that is indicated in our text. The fulfillment of the words may, at times, be in such striking interpositions of God's power that all can join in the cry: "Lo, this is our God...this is the Lord!" They may equally become true in spiritual experience, when God's people, in their waiting times, become so conscious of His presence that, in holy awe, souls feel: "Lo, this is our God...this is the Lord!" It is this, alas, that is too much missed in our meetings for worship. The godly minister has no more difficult, no more solemn, no more blessed task, than to lead his people out to meet God. And, before he preaches, he must bring each one into contact with Him. "We are now here in the presence of God"—these words of Cornelius show the way in which Peter's audience was prepared for the coming of the Holy Spirit. Waiting before God, waiting for God, and waiting on God are the conditions of God showing His presence.

A company of believers gathered with the one purpose, helping each other by little intervals of silence, to wait on God alone, opening the heart for whatever God may have of new discoveries of evil, of His will, of new openings in work or methods of work, would soon have reason to say: "Lo, this is our God; we have waited for Him, and He will save us: this is the Lord; we have waited for Him, we will be glad and rejoice in His salvation."

My soul, wait thou only upon God!

Chapter 19

AS A GOD OF JUDGMENT

"Yea, in the way of thy judgments, O Lord, have we waited for thee...for when thy judgments are in the earth, the inhabitants of the world will learn righteousness"—Isaiah 26:8,9.

"The Lord is a God of judgment: blessed are all they that wait for him"—Isaiah 30:18.

God is a God of mercy and a God of judgment. Mercy and judgment are forever together in His dealings. In the Flood, in the deliverance of Israel out of Egypt, in the overthrow of the Canaanites, we ever see mercy in the midst of judgment. In these, the inner circle of His own people, we see it, too. The judgment punishes the sin, while mercy saves the sinner. Or, rather, mercy saves the sinner, not in spite of, but by means of, the very judgment that came upon his sin. In waiting on God, we must beware of forgetting this—as we wait we must expect Him as a God of judgment.

"In the way of Thy judgments, O Lord, have we

waited for Thee." That will prove true in our inner experience. If we are honest in our longing for holiness—in our prayer to be wholly the Lord's— His holy presence will stir up and discover hidden sin. It will bring us very low in the bitter conviction of the evil of our nature, its opposition to God's law, and its inability to fulfill that law. The words will come true: "Who may abide the day of His coming, for He is like a refiner's fire." "Oh that Thou wouldest come down, as when the melting fire burneth!" In great mercy, God executes, within the soul, His judgments upon sin, as He makes it feel its wickedness and guilt. Many try to flee from these judgments. The soul that longs for God, and for deliverance from sin, bows under them in humility and in hope. In silence of soul, it says: "Arise, O Lord! and let Thine enemies be scattered. In the way of Thy judgments we have waited for Thee."

Let no one, who seeks to learn the blessed art of waiting on God, wonder if at first the attempt to wait on Him only reveals more of sin and darkness. Let no one despair because unconquered sins, evil thoughts, or great darkness appear to hide God's face. Was not, in His own beloved Son, the gift and bearer of His mercy on Calvary, the mercy as hidden and lost in the judgment? Oh, submit and sink down deep under the judgment of your every sin. Judgment prepares the way and breaks out in wonderful mercy. It is written: "Thou shalt be redeemed with judgment." Wait on God, in the faith that His tender mercy is working out His redemption in the midst of judgment. Wait for Him, He will be gracious to you.

There is another application still, one of unspeakable solemnity. We are expecting God, in the way of His judgments, to visit this earth: we are waiting for Him. What a thought! We know of these coming judgments. We know that there are tens of thousands of professing Christians who live on in carelessness, and who, if no change come, must perish under God's hand. Oh, will we not do our utmost to warn them, to plead with and for them, if God may have mercy on them! If we feel our lack of boldness, zeal, and power, will we not begin to wait on God more definitely and persistently as a God of judgment? Will we not ask Him to so reveal Himself in the judgments that are coming on our very friends, that we may be inspired with a new fear of Him and them, and constrained to speak and pray as never yet? Verily, waiting on God is not meant to be a spiritual self-indulgence. Its object is to let God and His holiness, Christ and the love that died on Calvary, the Spirit and fire that burns in heaven and came to earth, get possession of us, to warn and arouse men with the message that we are waiting for God in the way of His judgments. O Christian, prove that you really believe in the God of judgment!

My soul, wait thou only upon God!

Chapter 20

WHO WAITS ON US

"And therefore will the Lord wait, that he may be gracious unto you, and therefore will he be exalted, that he may have mercy upon you: for the Lord is a God of judgment: blessed are all they that wait for him"—Isaiah 30:18.

We must not only think of our waiting upon God, but also of what is more wonderful still, of God's waiting upon us. The vision of Him waiting on us will give new impulse and inspiration to our waiting upon Him. It will give us an unspeakable confidence that our waiting cannot be in vain. If He waits for us, then we may be sure that we are more than welcome —that He rejoices to find those He has been seeking for. Let us seek even now, at this moment, in the spirit of lowly waiting on God, to find out something of what it means. "Therefore will the Lord wait, that He may be gracious unto you." We will accept and echo back the message: "Blessed *are all they* that wait for Him."

Look up and see the great God upon His throne. He is love—an unceasing and inexpressible desire to communicate His own goodness and blessedness to all His creatures. He longs and delights to bless. He has inconceivably glorious purposes concerning every one of His children, by the power of His Holy Spirit, to reveal in them His love and power. He waits with all the longings of a father's heart. He waits that He may be gracious unto you. And, each time you come to wait upon Him, or seek to maintain in daily life the holy habit of waiting, you may look up and see Him ready to meet you. He will be waiting so that He may be gracious unto you. Yes, connect every exercise, every breath of the life of waiting, with faith's vision of your God waiting for you.

And if you ask: How is it, if He waits to be gracious, that even after I come and wait upon Him, He does not give the help I seek, but waits on longer and longer? There is a double answer. The one is this. God is a wise husbandman, "who waiteth for the precious fruit of the earth, and hath long patience for it." He cannot gather the fruit until it is ripe. He knows when we are spiritually ready to receive the blessing to our profit and His glory. Waiting in the sunshine of His love is what will ripen the soul for His blessing. Waiting under the cloud of trial, that breaks in showers of blessing, is as needful. Be assured that if God waits longer than you could wish, it is only to make the blessing doubly precious. God waited four thousand years, until the fullness of time, before He sent His Son. Our times are in His hands. He will avenge His elect speedily. He will make haste for our help, and not delay one hour too long.

The other answer points to what has been said before. The giver is more than the gift; God is more than the blessing. And, our being kept waiting on Him is the only way for our learning to find our life and joy *in Himself.* Oh, if God's children only knew what a glorious God they have, and what a privilege it is to be linked in fellowship with Him, then they would rejoice in Him! Even when He keeps them waiting, they will learn to understand better than ever. "Therefore will the Lord wait, that He may be gracious unto you." His waiting will be the highest proof of His graciousness.

"Blessed are all they that wait for Him." A queen has her ladies-in-waiting. The position is one of subordination and service, and yet it is considered one of the highest dignity and privilege, because a wise and gracious sovereign makes them companions and friends. What a dignity and blessedness to be attendants-in-waiting on the everlasting God, ever on the watch for every indication of His will or favor, ever conscious of His nearness, His goodness, and His grace! "The Lord is good to them that wait for Him." "Blessed are all they that wait for Him." Yes, it is blessed when a waiting soul and a waiting God meet each other. God cannot do His work without His and our waiting His time. Let waiting be our work, as it is His. And, if His waiting is nothing but goodness and graciousness, let ours be nothing but a rejoicing in that goodness, and a confident expectancy of that grace. And, let every thought of waiting become to us the simple expression of unmingled and unutterable blessedness, because it brings us to a God who waits that He may make Himself known to us perfectly as the gracious One.

My soul, wait thou only upon God!

Chapter 21

THE ALMIGHTY ONE

"They that wait on the Lord shall renew their strength; they shall mount up with wings as eagles; they shall run, and not be weary; and they shall walk, and not faint"—Isaiah 40:31.

Our waiting on God will depend greatly on our faith of what He is. In our text, we have the close of a passage in which God reveals Himself as the everlasting and almighty One. It is as that revelation enters into our soul that the waiting will become the spontaneous expression of what we know Him to be—a God altogether most worthy to be waited upon.

Listen to the words: "Why sayest thou, Jacob, my way is hid from the Lord? Why speakest thou as if God doth not hear or help?"

"Hast thou not known, hast thou not heard, that the Everlasting One, the Lord, the Creator of the ends of the earth, *fainteth not, neither is weary?"* So far from it: "He giveth power to the faint, and to them that have no might He increaseth strength. Even the youths"—"the glory of young men is their strength"—"even the youths shall faint, and the young men shall utterly fall." All that is deemed strong with man shall come to nothing. *"But* they that wait on the Lord," on the Everlasting One, who does not faint, neither is weary, they "shall renew their strength; they shall mount up with wings as eagles; they shall run, and"—listen now, they shall be strong with the strength of God, even as He *shall "not be weary;* and they shall walk, and," even as He, *"not faint."*

Yes, "they shall mount up with wings as eagles." You know what eagles' wings mean. The eagle is the king of birds; it soars the highest into the heavens. Believers are to live a heavenly life, in the very presence and love and joy of God. They are to live where God lives; they need God's strength to rise there. It will be given to them that wait on Him.

You know how the eagles' wings are obtained. Only in one way—by the eagle birth. You are born of God. You *have* the eagles' wings. You may not have known it; you may not have used them; but God can and will teach you how to use them.

You know how the eagles are taught the use of their wings. See yonder cliff rising a thousand feet out of the sea. See high up a ledge on the rock, where there is an eagle's nest with its treasure of two young eaglets. See the mother bird come and stir up her nest, and with her beak push the timid birds over the precipice. See how they flutter and fall and sink toward the depth. See now how she "fluttereth over her young, spreadeth abroad her wings, taketh them, beareth them on her wings" (Deuteronomy 32:11), and so, as they ride upon her wings, brings them to a place of safety. And so, she does once and again, each time casting them out over the precipice, and then again taking and carrying them. "So the Lord alone did lead him." Yes, the instinct of that eagle mother was God's gift, a single ray of that love in which the Almighty trains His people to mount as on eagles' wings.

He stirs up your nest. He disappoints your hopes. He brings down your confidence. He makes you fear and tremble, as all your strength fails, and you feel utterly weary and helpless. And, all the while He is spreading His strong wings for you to rest your weakness on, and offering His everlasting Creator-strength to work in you. And all He asks is that you sink down in your weariness and *wait on Him*. Allow Him in His Jehovah-strength to carry you as you ride upon the wings of His omnipotence.

Dear child of God, I pray you, lift up your eyes, and *behold your God!* Listen to Him who says that He "fainteth not, neither is weary," who promises that you too shall not faint or be weary, who asks nothing but this one thing, that you should *wait on Him*. And, let your answer be, With such a God, so mighty, so faithful, so tender,

My soul, wait thou only upon God!

Chapter 22

ITS CERTAINTY OF BLESSING

"Thou shalt know that I am the Lord: for they shall not be ashamed that wait for me"—Isaiah 49:23.

"Blessed are all they that wait for him"—Isaiah 30:18.

What promises! How God seeks to draw us to waiting on Him by the most positive assurance that it never can be in vain: "They shall not be ashamed that wait for Me." How strange that, though we should so often have experienced it, we are yet so slow to learn that this blessed waiting must and can be the very breath of our life—a continuous resting in God's presence and His love, an unceasing yielding of ourselves for Him to perfect His work in us. Let us once again listen and meditate, until our heart says with new conviction: *"Blessed are they* that wait for Him!"

We found in the prayer of Psalm 25: "Let none that wait on Thee be ashamed." The very prayer shows how we fear that it might be true. Let us listen to God's answer, until every fear is banished, and we send back to heaven the words God speaks, Yes, Lord, we believe what You say: *"All they* that wait for Me shall *not* be ashamed." "Blessed are *all they* that wait for Him."

The context of each of these two passages points us to times when God's Church was in great straits, and to human eyes there were no possibilities of deliverance. But, God interposes with His word of promise, and pledges His almighty power for the deliverance of His people. And, it is as the God who has Himself undertaken the work of their redemption that He invites them to wait on Him, and assures them that disappointment is impossible.

We, too, are living in days in which there is much in the state of the Church, with its profession and its formalism, that is indescribably sad. Amid all we praise God for, there is, alas, much to mourn over! Were it not for God's promises, we might well despair. But, in His promises the living God has given and bound Himself to us. He calls us to wait on Him. He assures us we will not be put to shame. Oh, that our hearts might learn to wait before Him, until He Himself reveals to us what His promises mean. In the promises, He reveals Himself in His hidden glory! We will be irresistibly drawn to wait on Him alone. God increase the company of those who say: "Our soul waiteth for the Lord: He is our help and our shield."

This waiting upon God on behalf of His Church

and people will depend greatly upon the place that waiting on Him has taken in our personal life. The mind may often have beautiful visions of what God has promised to do, and the lips may speak of them in stirring words, but these are not really the measure of our faith or power. No, it is what we really know of God in our personal experience, conquering the enemies within, reigning and ruling, revealing Himself in His holiness and power in our innermost being. It is this that will be the real measure of the spiritual blessing we expect from Him, and bring to our fellow-men.

It is as we know how blessed the waiting on God has become to our own souls, that we will confidently hope in the blessing to come on the Church around us. The keyword of all our expectations will be, He has said: "All they that wait on Me shall not be ashamed." From what He has done in us, we will trust Him to do mighty things around us. "Blessed are all they that wait for Him." Yes, blessed even now in the waiting. The promised blessings for ourselves, or for others, may tarry. The unutterable blessedness of knowing and having Him who has promised—the divine Blesser, the living Fountain of the coming blessings—is even now ours. Do let this truth acquire full possession of your souls, that waiting on God is itself the highest privilege of man, the highest blessedness of His redeemed child.

Even as the sunshine enters with its light and warmth, with its beauty and blessing, into every little blade of grass that rises upward out of the cold earth, so the everlasting God meets, in the greatness and the tenderness of His love, each waiting child, to shine in his heart "the light of the knowledge of the glory of God in the face of Jesus Christ." Read these words again, until your heart learns to know what God waits to do to you. Who can measure the difference between the great sun and that little blade of grass? And yet, the grass has all of the sun it can need or hold.

Do believe that in waiting on God, His greatness and your littleness suit and meet each other most wonderfully. Just bow in emptiness and poverty and utter weakness, in humility and meekness, and surrender to His will before His great glory, and be still. As you wait on Him, God draws near. He will reveal Himself as the God who will mightily fulfill His every promise. And, let your heart continually take up the song: "Blessed are all they that wait for Him."

My soul, wait thou only upon God!

Chapter 23

FOR UNLOOKED-FOR THINGS

"For since the beginning of the world men have not heard, nor perceived by the ear, neither hath the eye seen, O God, beside thee, what he hath prepared for him that waiteth for him"—Isaiah 64:4.

The American Standard Version has: *"Neither hath the eye seen a God besides thee, who worketh for him that waiteth for him."* In the Authorized Version, the thought is, that no eye has seen *the thing* which God has prepared. In the A.S.V., no eye has seen a God, besides our God, who works for him that waits for Him. To both, the two thoughts are common: that our place is to wait upon God, and that what the human heart cannot conceive will be revealed to us. The difference is: in the A.S.V. it is *the God* who works, in the A.V. *the thing* He is to work. In 1 Corinthians 2:9, the citation is in regard to the things which the Holy Spirit is to reveal, as in the A.V., and in this chapter we will keep to that.

The previous verses, especially Isaiah 63:15, refer

to the low state of God's people. The prayer has been poured out, "Look down from heaven" (v. 15). "Why hast Thou...hardened our heart from Thy fear? Return for Thy servants' sake" (v. 17). And 64:1, still more urgent, "Oh that Thou wouldest rend the heavens, that Thou wouldest come down...as when the melting fire burneth...to make Thy name known to Thy adversaries!" Then follows the plea from the past: "When Thou didst terrible things which we looked not for, Thou camest down, the mountains flowed down at Thy presence." "For" —this is now the faith that has been awakened by the thought of things we looked not for, He is still the same God—"neither hath the eye seen, O God, beside Thee, what He hath prepared for him that waiteth for Him."

God alone knows what He can do for His waiting people. As Paul expounds and applies it: "The things of God knoweth no man, save the Spirit of God." "But God hath revealed them to us by His Spirit."

The need of God's people, and the call for God's interposition, is as urgent in our days as it was in the time of Isaiah. There is now, as there was then, as there has been at all times, a few who seek after God with their whole heart. But, if we look at Christendom as a whole, at the state of the Church of Christ, there is infinite cause for beseeching God to rend the heavens and come down. Nothing but a special interposition of almighty power will avail. I fear we do not have a proper conception of what the so-called Christian world is in the sight of God. Unless God comes down "as when the melting fire burneth...to make known His name to His adversaries," our labors are comparatively fruitless.

Look at the ministry—how much it is in the wisdom of man and of literary culture—how little in demonstration of the Spirit and of power. Think of the unity of the body—how little there is of the manifestation of the power of a heavenly love binding God's children into one. Think of holiness—the holiness of Christlike humility and crucifixion to the world—how little the world sees that they have men among them who live in Christ in heaven, in whom Christ and heaven live.

What is to be done? There is only one thing. We must wait upon God. And what for? We must cry, with a cry that never rests, "Oh that Thou wouldest rend the heavens...come down, that the mountains might flow down at Thy presence." We must desire and believe, we must ask and expect, that God will do unlooked-for things. We must set our faith on a God of whom men do not know what He has prepared for them that wait for Him. The wonder-doing God, who can surpass all our expectations, must be the God of our confidence.

Yes, let God's people enlarge their hearts to wait on a God able to do exceeding abundantly above what we can ask or think. Let us band ourselves together as His elect who cry day and night to Him for things men have not seen. He is able to arise and to make His people a name and a praise in the earth.

"He will wait, that He may be gracious unto you;
blessed are all they that wait for Him."

My soul, wait thou only upon God!

Chapter 24

TO KNOW HIS GOODNESS

"The Lord is good unto them that wait for him"
—Lamentations 3:25.

"There is none good but God." "His goodness is in the heavens." "Oh how great is Thy goodness, which Thou hast laid up for them that fear Thee!" "O taste and see that the Lord is good!" And here is now the true way of entering into and rejoicing in this goodness of God—waiting upon Him. The Lord is good —even His children often do not know it, for they do not wait in quietness for Him to reveal it. But, to those who persevere in waiting, whose souls do wait, it will come true. One might think that it is just those who have to wait who might doubt it. But, this is only when they do not wait, but grow impatient. The truly waiting ones will all say: "The Lord is good unto them that wait for Him." If you want to fully know the goodness of God, give yourself more than ever to a life of waiting on Him.

At our first entrance into the school of waiting

upon God, the heart is mainly set on the blessings which we wait for. God graciously uses our need and desire for help to educate us for something higher than we were thinking of. We were seeking gifts; He, the Giver, longs to give Himself and to satisfy the soul with His goodness. It is just for this reason that He often withholds the gifts, and that the time of waiting is made so long. He is constantly seeking to win the heart of His child for Himself. He wishes that we would not only say, when He bestows the gift, How good is God! but that long before it comes, and even if it never comes, we should all the time be experiencing: *It is good* that a man should quietly wait. "The Lord *is good* to them that wait for Him."

What a blessed life the life of waiting then becomes, the continual worship of faith, adoring and trusting His goodness. As the soul learns its secret, every act or exercise of waiting becomes just a quiet entering into the goodness of God, to let it do its blessed work and satisfy our every need. And, every experience of God's goodness gives the work of waiting new attractiveness. Instead of only taking refuge in time of need, there comes a great longing to wait continually and all day. And, however duties and engagements occupy the time and the mind, the soul gets more familiar with the secret art of always waiting. Waiting becomes the habit and disposition, the very second nature and breath of the soul.

Dear Christian, begin to see that waiting is not one among a number of Christian virtues, to be thought of from time to time. But, it expresses that disposition which lies at the very root of the Christian life. It gives a higher value and a new power to our prayer and worship, to our faith and surrender, because it links us, in unalterable dependence, to God Himself. And, it gives us the unbroken enjoyment of the goodness of God: "The Lord is good unto them that wait for Him."

Let me stress once again that you must take time and trouble to cultivate this much needed element of the Christian life. We get too much second hand religion from the teaching of men. That teaching has great value, even as the preaching of John the Baptist sent his disciples away from himself to the living Christ, if it leads us to God Himself. What our faith needs is—*more of God.*

Many of us are too occupied with our work. As with Martha, the very service we want to render the Master separates us from Him. It is neither pleasing to Him nor profitable to ourselves. The more work, the more need of waiting upon God. The doing of God's will would then be, instead of exhausting, our meat and drink, our nourishment and refreshment and strength. "The Lord is good unto them that wait for Him." How good is known only by those who prove it in waiting on Him. How good none can fully tell but those who have proved Him to the utmost.

My soul, wait thou only upon God!

Chapter 25

QUIETLY

"It is good that a man should both hope and quietly wait for the salvation of the Lord"—Lamentations 3:26.

"Take heed, and be quiet: fear not, neither be faint-hearted." "In quietness and in confidence shall be your strength." Such words reveal to us the close connection between quietness and faith. They show us what a deep need there is of quietness, as an element of true waiting upon God. If we are to have our whole heart turned toward God, we must have it turned away from man, from all that occupies and interests, whether of joy or sorrow.

God is a being of such infinite greatness and glory, and our nature has become so estranged from Him, that it needs our whole heart and desires set upon Him, even in some little measure to know and receive Him. Everything that is not God, that excites our fears or stirs our efforts or awakens our hopes or makes us glad, hinders us in our perfect waiting on

Him. The message is one of deep meaning: "Take heed and be quiet"; "In quietness shall be your strength"; "It is good that a man should quietly wait."

Scripture abundantly testifies how the very thought of God in His majesty and holiness should silence us.

"The Lord is in His holy temple: let all the earth keep silence before Him" (Habakkuk 2:20).

"Hold thy peace at the presence of the Lord God" (Zephaniah 1:7).

"Be silent, O all flesh, before the Lord: for He is raised up out of His holy habitation" (Zechariah 2:13).

As long as the waiting on God is chiefly regarded as an end toward more effectual prayer, and the obtaining of our petitions, this spirit of perfect quietness will not be obtained. But, when it is seen that waiting on God is itself an unspeakable blessedness—one of the highest forms of fellowship with the Holy One—the adoration of Him in His glory will of necessity humble the soul into a holy stillness, making way for God to speak and reveal Himself. Then, it comes to the fulfillment of the precious promise, that all of self and self-effort will be humbled: "The haughtiness of man shall be brought down, and the Lord alone shall be exalted in that day."

Let everyone who wants to learn the art of waiting on God remember the lesson: "Take heed, and be quiet"; "It is good that a man quietly wait." Take time to be separate from all friends and all duties, all cares and all joys; time to be still and quiet before God. Take time not only to secure stillness from man and the world, but from self and its energy. Let the Word and prayer be very precious. But remember, even these may hinder the quiet waiting. The activity of the mind in studying the Word or giving expression to its thoughts in prayer, the activities of the heart, with its desires and hopes and fears, may so engage us that we do not come to the still waiting on the All-glorious One; our whole being is prostrate in silence before Him.

Though at first it may appear difficult to know how thus quietly to wait, with the activities of mind and heart for a time subdued, every effort after it will be rewarded. We will discover that it grows upon us, and the little season of silent worship will bring a peace and a rest that give a blessing not only in prayer, but all day.

"It is good that a man should...quietly wait for the salvation of the Lord." Yes, it is good. The quietness is the confession of our meekness. It will not be done with all our willing and running, with all our thinking and praying. We must receive it from God. It is the confession of our trust that our God will, in His time, come to our help—the quiet resting in Him alone. It is the confession of our desire to sink into our nothingness, and to let Him work and reveal Himself. Do let us wait quietly. In daily life, let there be, in the soul that is waiting for the great God to do His wondrous work, a quiet reverence, an abiding watching against too deep engrossment with

the world. Then, the whole character will come to bear the beautiful stamp: Quietly waiting for the salvation of God.

My soul, wait thou only upon God!

Chapter 26

IN HOLY EXPECTANCY

"Therefore will I look to the Lord; I will wait for the God of my salvation: my God will hear me"— Micah 7:7.

Have you ever read a little book, *Expectation Corners?* If not, get it. You will find in it one of the best sermons on our text. It tells of a king who prepared a city for some of his poor subjects. Not far from them were large storehouses, where everything they could need was supplied if they sent in their requests. But, on one condition—that they should be on the outlook for the answer, so that when the king's messengers came with the answer to their petitions, they should always be found waiting and ready to receive them. The sad story is told of one desponding person who never expected to get what he asked, because he was too unworthy. One day, he was taken to the king's storehouses, and there, to his amazement, he saw, with his address on them, all the packages that had been made up for him and sent.

There was the garment of praise and the oil of joy and the eyesalve and so much more. They had been to his door, but found it closed; he was not on the outlook. From that time on, he learned the lesson Micah would teach us today. I will "look to the Lord; I will wait for the God of my salvation; my God will hear me."

We have said more than once: Waiting for the answer to prayer is not the whole of waiting, but only a part. Today, we want to take in the blessed truth that it is a part, and a very important one. When we have special petitions, in connection with which we are waiting on God, our waiting must be very definitely in the confident assurance: "My God will hear me."

A holy, joyful expectancy is of the very essence of true waiting. And, this is not only true in reference to the many varied requests every believer has to make, but most especially to the one great petition which ought to be the chief thing every heart seeks for itself—that the life of God in the soul may have full sway. That Christ may be fully formed within, and that we may be filled to all the fullness of God. This is what God has promised. This is what God's people too little seek, very often because they do not believe it possible. This is what we ought to seek and dare to expect, because God is able and waiting to work it in us.

But, God Himself must work it. And for this end our working must cease. We must see how entirely it is to be the faith of the operation of God who raised

Jesus from the dead—just as much as the resurrection, the perfecting of God's life in our souls is to be directly His work. And, waiting has to become, more than ever, a tarrying before God in stillness of soul, counting upon Him who raises the dead and calls the things that are not as though they were.

Just notice how the threefold use of the name of God in our text points us to Himself as the one from whom alone is our expectation. "I (will) look to the Lord; I will wait for the God of my salvation: my God will hear me." Everything that is salvation, everything that is good and holy, must be the direct, mighty work of God Himself within us. In every moment of a life in the will of God, there must be the immediate operation of God. And, the one thing I have to do is this: to look to the Lord; to wait for the God of my salvation; to hold fast the confident assurance, "My God will hear me."

God says: "Be still, and know that I am God."

There is no stillness like that of the grave. In the grave of Jesus, in the fellowship of His death, in death to self with its own will and wisdom, its own strength and energy, there is rest. As we cease from self, and our soul becomes still to God, God will arise and show Himself. "Be still, and know," then you will know "that I am God." There is no stillness like the stillness Jesus gives when He speaks. "Peace, be still." In Christ, in His death, *in His life,* in His perfected redemption, the soul may be still, and God will come in, take possession, and do His perfect work.

My soul, be thou still only unto God!

113

Chapter 27

FOR REDEMPTION

"Simeon...was just and devout, waiting for the consolation of Israel: and the Holy Ghost was upon him...Anna, a prophetess...spake of him to all them that looked for redemption in Jerusalem" —Luke 2:25,36,38.

Here we have the mark of a waiting believer. *Just,* righteous in all his conduct; *devout,* devoted to God, ever walking as in His presence; *waiting for the consolation of Israel,* looking for the fulfillment of God's promises: *and the Holy Ghost was on him.* In the devout waiting, he had been prepared for the blessing. And Simeon was not the only one. Anna spoke to all that looked for redemption in Jerusalem. This was the one mark, amid surrounding formalism and worldliness, of a godly band of men and women in Jerusalem. They were waiting on God, looking for His promised redemption.

And now that the consolation of Israel has come, and the redemption has been accomplished, do we still need to wait? We do indeed. But, will not our waiting, who look back to it as come, differ greatly from those who looked forward to it as coming? It will, especially in two aspects. We now wait on God in the full power of the redemption; and we wait for its full revelation.

Our waiting is now in the full power of the redemption. Christ spoke: "In that day ye shall know that ye are *in Me*. Abide in Me." The Epistles teach us to present ourselves to God "as indeed dead to sin, and alive to God *in Christ Jesus*"; "blessed with all spiritual blessings in heavenly places *in Christ Jesus.*" Our waiting on God may now be in the wonderful consciousness, and maintained by the Holy Spirit within us, that we are accepted in the Beloved, that the love that rests on Him rests on us, that we are living in that love, in the very nearness and presence and sight of God.

The old saints took their stand on the Word of God, and waiting, hoping on that Word, we rest on the Word, too—but, oh, under what exceedingly greater privileges, as one with Christ Jesus! In our waiting on God, let this be our confidence: in Christ we have access to the Father. How sure, therefore, we may be that our waiting cannot be in vain.

Our waiting differs, too, in this, that while they waited for a redemption to come, we see it accomplished and now wait for its revelation *in us*. Christ not only said, Abide in Me, but also *I in you.* The Epistles not only speak of us *in Christ,* but of Christ *in us,* as the highest mystery of redeeming love. As

116

we maintain our place in Christ day by day, God waits to reveal Christ in us, in such a way that He is formed in us, that His mind and disposition and likeness acquire form and substance in us, so that by each it can in truth be said, "Christ liveth in me."

My life in Christ up there in heaven and Christ's life in me down here on earth—these two are the complement of each other. And, the more my waiting on God is marked by the living faith *I in Christ,* the more the heart thirsts for and claims the Christ in me. And, the waiting on God, which began with special needs and prayer, will increasingly be concentrated, as far as our personal life is concerned, on this one thing: Lord, reveal Thy redemption fully in me; let Christ live in me.

Our waiting differs from that of the old saints in the place we take, and the expectations we entertain. But, at root it is the same: waiting on God, from whom alone is our expectation.

Learn one lesson from Simeon and Anna. How utterly impossible it was for them to do anything toward the great redemption—toward the birth of Christ or His death. *It was God's work. They could do nothing but wait.* Are we as absolutely helpless in regard to the revelation of Christ in us? We are indeed. God did not work out the great redemption in Christ as a whole, and leave its application in detail to us.

The secret thought that it is so, is the root of all our feebleness. The revelation of Christ in every individual believer, and in each one the daily revelation, step by step and moment by moment, is as much the work of God's omnipotence as the birth or resurrection of Christ. Until this truth enters and fills us, and we feel that we are just as dependent upon God for each moment of our life in the enjoyment of redemption as they were in their waiting for it, our waiting upon God will not bring its full blessing. The sense of utter and absolute helplessness, the confidence that God can and will do all—these must be the marks of our waiting as of theirs. As gloriously as God proved Himself to them the faithful and wonder-working God, He will to us, too.

My soul, wait thou only upon God!

Chapter 28

FOR THE COMING OF HIS SON

"Be . . . ye yourselves like unto men that wait for their Lord"—Luke 12:36.

"Until the appearing of our Lord Jesus Christ: which in his own time he shall show, who is the blessed and only Potentate, the King of kings, and Lord of lords"—1 Timothy 6:14,15 (A.S.V.).

"Turned to God from idols to serve the living and true God; and to wait for his Son from heaven"—1 Thessalonians 1:9,10.

Waiting on God in heaven, and waiting for His Son from heaven, these two God has joined together and no man may put them asunder. The waiting on God for His presence and power in daily life will be the only true preparation for waiting for Christ in humility and true holiness. The waiting for Christ coming from heaven to take us to heaven will give the waiting on God its true tone of hopefulness and joy. The Father, who, in His own time, will reveal His Son from heaven, is the God who, as we wait on

Him, prepares us for the revelation of His Son. The present life and the coming glory are inseparably connected in God and in us.

There is sometimes a danger of separating them. It is always easier to be engaged with the Christianity of the past or the future than to be faithful in the Christianity of today. As we look to what God has done in the past, or will do in time to come, the personal claim of present duty and present submission to His working may be avoided. Waiting on God must always lead to waiting for Christ as the glorious consummation of His work. And, waiting for Christ must always remind us of the duty of waiting upon God as our only proof that the waiting for Christ is in spirit and in truth.

There is such a danger of our being more occupied with the things that are coming than *with Him* who is to come. There is such scope in the study of coming events for imagination and reason and human ingenuity, that nothing but deeply humble waiting on God can save us from mistaking the interest and pleasure of intellectual study for the true love of Him and His appearing. All you that say you wait for Christ's coming, *be sure that you wait on God now.* All you who seek to wait on God now to reveal His Son in you, see to it that you do so as men waiting for the revelation of His Son from heaven. The hope of that glorious appearing will strengthen you in waiting upon God for what He is to do in you now. The same omnipotent love that is to reveal that glory is working in you even now to prepare you for it.

"The blessed hope and appearing of the glory of the great God and our Saviour Jesus Christ" (Titus 2:13), is one of the great bonds of union given to God's Church throughout the ages. "He shall come to be glorified in His saints, and to be marveled at in all them that believe." Then, we will all meet, and the unity of the body of Christ be seen in its divine glory. It will be the meeting place and the triumph of divine love. Jesus receiving His own and presenting them to the Father. His own meeting Him and worshipping, in speechless love, that blessed face. His own meeting each other in the ecstasy of God's own love. Let us wait, long for, and love the appearing of our Lord and heavenly Bridegroom. Tender love to Him and tender love to each other is the true and only bridal spirit.

I am very afraid that this is sometimes forgotten. A beloved brother in Holland was speaking about the expectancy of faith being the true sign of the bride. I ventured to express a doubt. An unworthy bride, about to be married to a prince, might only be thinking of the position and the riches that she was to receive. The expectancy of faith might be strong, and true love utterly lacking. It is not when we are most occupied with prophetic subjects, but when in humility and love we are clinging close to our Lord and His brethren, that we are in the bride's place. Jesus refuses to accept our love except as it is love to His disciples. Waiting for His coming means waiting for the glorious coming manifestation of the unity of the body, while we seek here to maintain that unity in humility and love. Those who love most are the most ready for His coming. Love to each other is the life and beauty of His Bride, the Church.

And how is this to be brought about? Beloved child of God, if you want to learn how to properly wait for His Son from heaven, live even now waiting on God in heaven. Remember how Jesus lived ever waiting on God. He could do nothing of Himself. It was God who perfected His Son through suffering and then exalted Him. It is God alone who can give you the deep spiritual life of one who is really waiting for His Son: wait on God for it. Waiting for Christ Himself is so different from waiting for things that may come to pass! The latter any Christian can do; the former, God must work in you every day by His Holy Spirit. Therefore, all you who wait on God, look to Him for grace to wait for His Son from heaven in the Spirit which is from heaven. And, you who want to wait for His Son, wait on God continually to reveal Christ in you.

The revelation of Christ in us as it is given to them who wait upon God is the true preparation for the full revelation of Christ in glory.

My soul, wait thou only upon God!

Chapter 29

FOR THE PROMISE OF THE FATHER

"He charged them not to depart from Jerusalem, but to wait for the promise of the Father"—Acts 1:4 (A.S.V.).

In speaking of the saints in Jerusalem at Christ's birth—with Simeon and Anna—we saw how the call to waiting is no less urgent now though the redemption they waited for is come, than it was then. We wait for the full revelation in us of what came to them, but what they could scarcely comprehend. Even so, it is with waiting for the promise of the Father. In one sense, the fulfillment can never come again as it came at Pentecost. In another sense, and that in as deep a reality as with the first disciples, we need to wait daily for the Father to fulfill His promise in us.

The Holy Spirit is not a person distinct from the Father in the way two persons on earth are distinct. The Father and the Spirit are never without or separate from each other. The Father is always in the Spirit; the Spirit works nothing but as the Father works in Him. Each moment, the same Spirit that is in us is in God, too. And, he who is most full of the Spirit will be the first to wait on God most earnestly, to further fulfill His promise, and still strengthen him mightily by His Spirit in the inner man. The Spirit in us is not a power at our disposal. Nor is the Spirit an independent power, acting apart from the Father and the Son. The Spirit is *the real living presence and the power of the Father* working in us. Therefore, it is he who knows that the Spirit is in him who waits on the Father for the full revelation and experience of the Spirit's indwelling. It is he who waits for His increase and abounding more and more.

See this in the apostles. They were filled with the Spirit at Pentecost. When they, not long after, on returning from the Council where they had been forbidden to preach, prayed afresh for boldness to speak in His name—a fresh coming down of the Holy Spirit was the Father's fresh fulfillment of His promise.

At Samaria, by the Word and the Spirit, many had been converted, and the whole city was filled with joy. At the apostles' prayer, the Father once again fulfilled the promise. Even so to the waiting company—"We are all here before God"—in Cornelius' house. And so, too, in Acts 13. It was when men, filled with the Spirit, prayed and fasted, that the promise of the Father was afresh fulfilled, and the leading of the Spirit was given from heaven: "Separate me Barnabas and Saul."

So also we find Paul, in Ephesians, praying for those who have been sealed with the Spirit, that God would grant them the spirit of illumination. And later on, that He would grant them, according to the riches of His glory, to be strengthened with might by the Spirit in the inner man.

The Spirit given at Pentecost was not something that God failed with in heaven, and sent out of heaven to earth. God does not, cannot, give away anything in that manner. When He gives grace or strength or life, He gives it by giving Himself to work it—it is all inseparable from Himself. Much more so is the Holy Spirit. He is God, present and working in us. The true position in which we can count upon that working with an unceasing power is as we, praising for what we have, still unceasingly wait for the Father's promise to be still more mightily fulfilled.

What new meaning and promise does this give to our life of waiting! It teaches us to continually keep the place where the disciples tarried at the footstool of the Throne. It reminds us that, as helpless as they were to meet their enemies, or to preach to Christ's enemies until they were endued with power, we, too, can only be strong in the life of faith, or the work of love, as we are in direct communication with God and Christ. They must maintain the life of the Spirit in us. This assures us that the omnipotent God will, through the glorified Christ, work in us a power which can bring unexpected things to pass, impossible things. Oh, what the Church will be able to do when her individual members learn to live their lives waiting on God! When together, with all of self and the world sacrificed in the fire of love, they unite in waiting with one accord for the promise of the Father, once so gloriously fulfilled, but still unexhausted!

Come and let each of us be still in the presence of the inconceivable grandeur of this prospect: the Father waiting to fill the Church with the Holy Spirit. And willing to fill *me,* let each one say.

With this faith, let a hush and a holy fear come over the soul, as it waits in stillness to take it all in. And, let life increasingly become a deep joy in the hope of the ever fuller fulfillment of the Father's promise.

My soul, wait thou only upon God!

Chapter 30

CONTINUALLY

"Therefore turn thou to thy God: keep mercy and judgment and wait on thy God continually" —Hosea 12:6.

Continuity is one of the essential elements of life. Interrupt it for a single hour in a man, and it is lost; he is dead. Continuity, unbroken and ceaseless, is essential to a healthy Christian life. God wants me to be, and God waits to make me, I want to be, and I wait on Him to make me, every moment, what He expects of me—what is well-pleasing in His sight. If waiting on God is the essence of true faith, the maintenance of the spirit of entire dependence must be continuous. The call of God, "Wait on thy God continually," must be accepted and obeyed. There may be times of special waiting: the disposition and habit of soul must be there unchangeably and uninterrupted.

This continual waiting is indeed a necessity. To those who are content with a feeble Christian life, it appears to be a luxury beyond what is essential to be a good Christian. But, all who are praying the prayer, "Lord, make me as holy as a pardoned sinner can be made! Keep me as near to Thee as it is possible for me to be! Fill me as full of Thy love as Thou art willing to do!" feel at once that it is something that must be had. They feel that there can be no unbroken fellowship with God, no full abiding in Christ, no maintaining of victory over sin and readiness for service, without waiting continually on the Lord.

The continual waiting is a possibility. Many think that with the duties of life it is out of the question. They cannot always be thinking of it. Even when they wish to, they forget.

They do not understand that it is a matter of the heart, and that what the heart is full of, occupies it, even when the thoughts are otherwise engaged. A father's heart may be continuously filled with intense love and longing for a sick wife or child at a distance, even though pressing business requires all his thoughts. When *the heart* has learned how entirely powerless it is for one moment to keep itself or bring forth any good, when it has learned how surely and truly God will keep it, when it has, in despair of itself, accepted God's promise to do for it the impossible, it learns to rest in God. In the midst of occupations and temptations, it can wait continually.

This waiting is a promise. God's commands are enablings. Gospel precepts are all promises, a revelation of what our God will do for us. When you first begin waiting on God, it is with frequent intermission and failure. But, do believe God is watching over you in love and secretly strengthening you in it. There are times when waiting appears like just losing time, but it is not so. Waiting, even in darkness, is unconscious advance, because it is God you have to do with, and He is working in you. God, who calls you to wait on Him, sees your feeble efforts, and works it in you. Your spiritual life is in no respect your own work; as little as you begin it, can you continue it. It is God's Spirit who has begun the work in you of waiting upon God. He will enable you to wait continually.

Waiting continually will be met and rewarded by God Himself working continually. We are coming to the end of our lessons. I hope that you and I might learn one thing: God must, God will work continually. He ever does work continually, but the experience of it is hindered by unbelief. But, He, who by His Spirit teaches you to wait continually, will bring you to also experience how, as the Everlasting One, His work is never-ceasing. In the love and the life and the work of God, there can be no break, no interruption.

Do not limit God in this by your thoughts of what may be expected. Do fix your eyes upon this one truth: in His very nature, God, as the only Giver of life, *cannot do otherwise than every moment work in His child.* Do not look only at the one side: "If I wait continually, God will work continually." No, look at the other side. Place God first and say, *"God works continually; every moment I may wait on Him continually."* Take time until the vision of your God working continually, without one moment's intermission, fills your being. Your waiting continually will then come of itself. Full of trust and joy, the holy habit of the soul will be:

"On Thee do I wait *all the day."* The Holy Spirit will keep you ever waiting.

My soul, wait thou only upon God!

Chapter 31

ONLY

"My soul, wait thou only upon God; for my expectation is from him. He only is my rock and my salvation"—Psalm 62:5,6.

It is possible to be waiting continually on God, but not *only* upon Him. There may be other secret confidences intervening and preventing the blessing that was expected. And so the word *only* must come to throw its light on the path to the fullness and certainty of blessing. "My soul, wait thou *only* upon God. . . . He *only* is my rock."

Yes, "My soul, wait thou only upon God." There is but one God, but one source of life and happiness for the heart; "He *only* is my rock"; "my soul, wait thou *only* upon (God)." You desire to be good, "There is none good but God," and there is no possible goodness but what is received directly from Him. You have sought to be holy: "There is none holy but the Lord," and there is no holiness but what He by His Spirit of holiness every moment breathes in you. You would gladly live and work for God and

His Kingdom, for men and their salvation. Hear how He says: "The Everlasting God, the Creator of the ends of the earth. He alone fainteth not, neither is weary. He giveth power to the faint, and to them that have no might He increaseth strength. They that wait upon the Lord shall renew their strength." He only is God; He only is your Rock: "My soul, wait thou only upon God."

"My soul, wait *thou* only upon God." You will not find many who can help you in this. There will be enough of your brethren to draw you to put trust in churches and doctrines, in schemes and plans and human appliances, in means of grace and divine appointments. But, "my soul, wait thou only upon God" Himself. His most sacred appointments become a snare when trusted in. The brazen serpent becomes Nehushtan; the ark and the temple a vain confidence. Let the living God alone, none and nothing but He, be your hope.

"*My soul,* wait thou only upon God." Eyes and hands and feet, mind and thought, may have to be intently engaged in the duties of this life. "*My soul,* wait thou only upon God." You are an immortal spirit, created not for this world but for eternity and for God. O my soul, realize your destiny. Know your privilege, and "wait thou *only upon God.*" Let not the interest of spiritual thoughts and exercises deceive you; they very often take the place of waiting upon God. "My soul, wait *thou,*" your very self, your innermost being, with all its power, "wait thou only upon God." God is for you; you are for God.

Wait only upon Him.

Yes, "My soul, wait thou *only* upon God." Beware of two great enemies—the world and self. Beware of allowing any earthly satisfaction or enjoyment, however innocent it appears, keep you back from saying, "I will go to God, my exceeding joy." Remember and study what Jesus says about denying self, "Let a man deny himself." Tersteegen says: "The saints deny themselves in everything." Pleasing self in little things may be strengthening it to assert itself in greater things.

"My soul, wait thou *only* upon God." Let Him be all your salvation and all your desire. Say continually and with an undivided heart: "From Him cometh my expectation. He only is my Rock; I shall not be moved." Whatever your spiritual or temporal needs are, whatever the desire or prayer of your heart, whatever your interest in connection with God's work in the Church or the world—in solitude or in the rush of the world, in public worship or other gatherings of the saints, "My soul, wait thou *only* upon God." Let your expectations be from Him alone. "He only is my (thy) rock."

"My soul, wait thou only upon God." Never forget the two foundation truths on which this blessed waiting rests. If you are ever inclined to think this "waiting only" too hard or too high, they will recall you at once. They are: your absolute helplessness; the absolute sufficiency of your God. Oh, enter deeply into the entire sinfulness of all that is of self, and do not think of letting self have anything to say one single moment. Enter deeply into your utter and unceasing inability to ever change what is evil in you, or to bring forth anything that is spiritually good. Enter deeply into your relationship of dependence on God, to receive from Him every moment what He gives. Enter deeper still into His covenant of redemption, with His promise to restore more gloriously than ever what you have lost. And, by His Son and Spirit, He will unceasingly give you His actual divine presence and power. And thus, wait upon your God continually and only.

"My soul, wait thou only upon God." No words can tell, no heart can conceive, the riches of the glory of this mystery of the Father and of Christ. Our God, in the infinite tenderness and omnipotence of His love, waits to be our life and joy. Oh, my soul, let it no longer be necessary that I repeat the words, "Wait upon God." But, let all that is in me rise and sing: "Truly my soul waiteth upon God. On Thee do I wait all the day."

My soul, wait thou only upon God!

MOMENT BY MOMENT

I the Lord do keep it: I will water it every moment

Dying with Jesus, by death reckoning mine;
Living with Jesus, a new life divine;
Looking to Jesus till glory doth shine,
Moment by moment, O Lord, I am Thine.

Chorus: Moment by moment I'm kept in His love;
Moment by moment I've life from above;
Looking to Jesus till glory doth shine;
Moment by moment, O Lord, I am Thine.

Never a battle with wrong for the right,
Never a contest that He doth not fight;
Lifting above us His banner so white,
Moment by moment, I'm kept in His sight.

Never a trial that He is not there,
Never a burden that He doth not bear,
Never a sorrow that He doth not share,
Moment by moment I'm under His care;

Never a heartache, and never a groan,
Never a teardrop and never a moan;
Never a danger but there on the throne,
Moment by moment He thinks of His own.

Never a weakness that He doth not feel,
Never a sickness that He cannot heal;
Moment by moment, in woe or in weal,
Jesus, my Saviour, abides with me still.

ABOUT THE AUTHOR

Andrew Murray (1828-1917) was an amazingly prolific Christian writer. He lived and ministered as both a pastor and author from the Cape of South Africa.

The earliest of his writings were actually an extension of his pastoral work. He wrote to give daily practical help to many of the people in his congregation who lived out in the farming communities and could only come into town for church services on rare occasions. As he wrote these books of instruction, Andrew Murray adopted the practice of placing many of his more devotional books into thirty-one separate readings to correspond with the days of the month.

At the age of seventy-eight, Murray resigned from the pastorate and devoted most of his time to his manuscripts. He continued to write profusely, moving from one book to the next with an intensity of purpose and a zeal that few men of God have ever equaled. He often said of himself, rather humorously, that he was like a hen about to hatch an egg; he was restless and unhappy until he got the burden of the message off his mind.

During these later years, after hearing of pocket-sized paperbacks, Andrew Murray immediately began to write books to be published in that fashion. He thought it was a splendid way to have the teachings of the Christian life at your fingertips, where they could be carried around and read at any time of the day.

Countless persons the world over have hailed Andrew Murray as their spiritual father and given credit for much of their Christian growth to the influence of his priceless devotional books.

ANOTHER POWERFUL Book

from Whitaker House

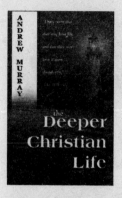

The Deeper Christian Life

Andrew Murray

God intends you to have all the blessings of His
storehouse, including His free favor, peace in the
storms of life, and the power of the Holy Spirit. As your
Christian walk is transformed into the happy way of life
that God intends for you, you will realize the desires of
your heart and the joy of God's presence.

ISBN: 0-88368-298-2 • Pocket • 112 pages